POEMS.

POEMS AND PARODIES

BY

PHŒBE CAREY.

BOSTON:
TICKNOR, REED, AND FIELDS.
M DCCC LIV.

CAMBRIDGE:
METCALF AND COMPANY, PRINTERS TO THE UNIVERSITY.

CONTENTS.

PARODIES.

ENTERING HEAVEN.

Softly part away the tresses
  From her forehead of white clay,
And across her quiet bosom
  Let her pale hands lightly lay;
Never idly in her lifetime
  Were they folded thus away.

She hath lived a life of labor,
  She has done with toil and care,
She hath lived a life of sorrow,
  She has nothing more to bear,
And the lips that never murmured
  Never more shall move in prayer.

You who watched with me beside her,
As her last of nights went by,
Know how calmly she assured us
That her hour was drawing nigh;
How she told us, sweetly smiling,
She was glad that she could die.

Many times from off the pillow
Lifting up her face to hear,
She had seemed to watch and listen,
Half in hope and half in fear,
Often asking those about her
If the day were drawing near.

Till at last, as one aweary,
To herself she murmured low,
"Could I see him, could I bless him
Only once before I go;
If he knew that I was dying,
He would come to me, I know."

Drawing then my head down gently,
Till it lay beside her own,
Said she, "Tell him in his anguish,
When he finds that I am gone,

That the bitterness of dying
  Was to leave him here alone.

"Leave me now, my dear ones, leave me,
  You are wearied now, I know;
You have all been kind and watchful,
  You can do no more below,
And if none I love are near me,
  'T will be easier to go.

"Let your warm hands chill not slipping
  From my fingers' icy tips,
Be there not the touch of kisses
  On my uncaressing lips,
Let no kindness see the darkening
  Of my eyes' last, long eclipse.

"Never think of me as lying
  By the dismal mould o'erspread,
But about the soft white pillow
  Folded underneath my head;
And of summer flowers weaving
  A rich broidery o'er my bed.

"Think of the immortal spirit
  Living up above the sky,

And of how my face, there wearing
  Light of immortality,
Looking earthward, is o'erleaning
  The white bastions of the sky."

Stilling then, with one last effort,
  All her weakness and her woe,
She seemed wrapt in pleasant visions
  But to wait her time to go;
For she never after midnight
  Spoke of any thing below, —

But kept murmuring very softly
  Of cool streams and pleasant bowers,
Of a pathway going up brightly,
  Where the fields were white with flowers;
And at daybreak she had entered
  On a better life than ours.

OUR BABY.

WHEN the morning, half in shadow,
Ran along the hill and meadow,
And with milk-white fingers parted
Crimson roses, golden-hearted;
Opening over ruins hoary
Every purple morning-glory,
And outshaking from the bushes
Singing larks and pleasant thrushes; —
That 's the time our little baby,
Strayed from Paradise, it may be,
Came with eyes like heaven above her:
O, we could not choose but love her!

Not enough of earth for sinning,
Always gentle, always winning,

Never needing our reproving,
Ever lovely, ever loving;
Starry eyes and sunset tresses,
White arms, made for light caresses,
Lips, that knew no word of doubting,
Often kissing, never pouting;
Beauty even in completeness,
Overfull in childish sweetness; —
That 's the way our little baby,
Far too pure for earth, it may be,
Seemed to us, who while about her
Deemed we could not do without her.

When the morning, half in shadow,
Ran along the hill and meadow,
And with milk-white fingers parted
Crimson roses, golden-hearted;
Opening over ruins hoary
Every purple morning-glory,
And outshaking from the bushes
Singing larks and pleasant thrushes; —
That 's the time our little baby,
Pining here for heaven, it may be,
Turning from our bitter weeping,
Closed her eyes as when in sleeping,

And her white hands on her bosom
Folded like a summer blossom.

Now the litter she doth lie on,
Strewed with roses, bear to Zion ;
Go, as past a pleasant meadow
Through the valley of the shadow ;
Take her softly, holy angels,
Past the ranks of God's evangels,
Past the saints and martyrs holy,
To the Earth-born, meek and lowly ;
We would have our precious blossom
Softly laid in Jesus' bosom.

THE OUTCAST.

She died at the middle of night:
And brother nor sister, lover nor friend,
Came not near her their aid to lend,
Ere the spirit took its flight.

She died at the middle of night:
Food and raiment she had no more,
And the fire had died on the hearth before, —
'T was a pitiful, pitiful sight.

She died at the middle of night:
No napkin pressed back the parted lips ;
No weeper, watching the eyes' eclipse,
Covered them up from sight.

She died at the middle of night:
And there was no taper beside the dead,
But the stars, through the broken roof o'erhead,
Shone with a solemn light.

She died at the middle of night:
And the winter snow spread a winding-sheet
Over the body from head to feet,
Dainty, and soft, and white.

She died at the middle of night:
But if she heard, ere her hour was o'er,
"I have not condemned thee, — sin no more,"
She lives where the day is bright.

THE LIFE OF TRIAL.

I AM glad her life is over,
  Glad that all her trials are past;
For her pillow was not softened
  Down with roses to the last.

When sharp thorns choked up the pathway
  Where she wandered sad and worn,
Never kind hand pressed them backward,
  So her feet were pierced and torn.

And when life's stern course of duty
  Through the fiery furnace ran,
Never saw she one beside her,
  Like unto the Son of Man.

Ere the holy dew of baptism
  Cooled her aching forehead's heat,
Heaviest waters of affliction
  Many times had touched her feet.

Long for her deliverance waiting,
  Clung she to the cross in vain;
With an agonizing birth-cry
  Was her spirit born again.

And her path grew always rougher,
  Wearier, wearier, still she trod,
Till, through gates of awful anguish,
  She went in at last to God!

DEATH OF A FRIEND.

WHERE leaves by bitter winds are heaped
  In the deep hollows, damp and cold,
And the light snow-shower, silently,
  Is falling on the yellow mould,

Sleeps one who was our friend, below ; —
  With meek hands folded on her breast,
When the first flowers of summer died,
  We softly laid her down to rest.

By her were blessings freely strewn,
  As roses by the summer's breath ;
Yet nothing in her perfect life
  Was half so lovely as her death.

In the meek beauty of a faith
  Which few have ever proved like her,
She shrunk not even when she felt
  The chill breath of the sepulchre.

Heavier, and heavier still, she leaned
  Upon His arm who died to save,
As step by step he led her down
  To the still chamber of the grave.

'T was at the midnight's solemn watch
  She sunk to slumber, calm and deep :
The golden fingers of the dawn
  Shall never wake her from that sleep.

From him who was her friend below,
  She turned to meet her Heavenly Guide ;
And the sweet children of her love,
  She left them sleeping when she died.

Her last of suns went calmly down,
  And when the morn rose bright and clear,
Hers was a holier Sabbath-day
  Than that which dawned upon us here.

CHALMERS.

As the red lights down in the water,
  When a boat shoots into the sea,
Or a star through the thin blue ether,
  He vanished silently.

Not the counsel of ghostly fathers
  Showed him the way he trod,
Not the picture of saints and martyrs,
  Nor the smile of the Mother of God.

Not the love-lighted brows of kindred,
  Nor the words of a faithful friend,
Opened up the way to his vision,
  And cheered him to the end.

As a God-fearing man, and holy,
He had passed through the snares beneath,
And he needed no aid to strengthen
His soul in the hour of death.

The steps of his faith were planted
Where the waves in vain might beat,
While the waters of death rose darkly,
And closed around his feet.

Not the "Save, or I perish!" of Peter,
Was his, as he faintly trod,
But the trust of that first blest martyr,
Falling asleep in God.

CHANGES.

UNDER the evening splendor
Of spring's sweet skies,
Learned I love's lesson tender,
From the maiden's eyes.

When the stars, like lovers meeting,
In the blue appeared,
And my heart, tumultuous beating,
Hoped and feared, —

Then the passion, long dissembled,
My lip made known,
And the hand of the maiden trembled
In my own, —

Till the tears that gushed unbidden,
    Unrepressed,
And the crimson blush, were hidden
    On my breast.

And there in that vale elysian,
    Through the summer bland,
We walked in a trancèd vision,
    Hand in hand.

There the evening shadows found us
    Side by side,
While the glorious roses round us
    Bloomed and died.

And when the bright sun, waning,
    Dimly burned, —
When the wind, with sad complaining,
    In the valley mourned, —

When the bridal roses faded
    In her hair,
And her brow was sweetly shaded
    With a thought of care, —

Then with heart still fondly thrilling,
  But with calmer bliss,
From the lip no more unwilling
  I claimed the kiss.

Then our dreams, with love o'erladen,
  Were verified,
And dearer to me than the maiden
  Grew the bride.

But when the dead leaves drifted
  In that valley low,
And down from the cold sky sifted
  The noiseless snow, —

Where the hearts of the faithful moulder
  With the dead,
They made her a pillow colder
  Than the bridal bed.

And there at the spring's returning,
  With the summer's glow,
When the autumn's sun is burning,
  In the winter's snow, —

With the ghosts of the dim past ever
    Gliding round,
Walk I in that vale, as a river
    That makes no sound.

DEATH SCENE.

Dying, still slowly dying,
As the hours of night wore by,
She had lain since the light of sunset
Was red on the evening sky, —

Till after the middle watches,
As we softly near her trod,
When her soul from its prison fetters
Was loosed by the hand of God.

One moment her pale lips trembled
With the triumph she might not tell,
As the light of the life immortal
On her spirit's vision fell.

Then the look of rapture faded,
  And the beautiful smile waxed faint,
As that in some convent picture
  On the face of a dying saint.

And we felt in the lonesome midnight,
  As we sat by the silent dead,
What a light on the path going downward
  The steps of the righteous shed ; —

When we thought how with feet unshrinking
  She came to the Jordan's tide,
And, taking the hand of the Saviour,
  Went up on the heavenly side !

OUR FRIEND.

We tried to win her from her grief,
  To soothe her great despair;
We showed her how the starry flowers
  Were growing everywhere, —
The starry flowers she used to braid
  At evening in her hair.

We told her how our hearts, for her,
  Beat mournfully and low;
How lines were deepening, day by day,
  Across her father's brow;
And how her little brother drooped, —
  He had no playmate now.

And then she spoke of weary nights
  Of dull and sleepless pain,
And how she grieved that loving friends
  Should plead with her in vain ;
And hoped that when the summer came
  She should be well again.

Still softly singing to herself
  Sad words of plaintive rhyme,
She always watched the sun's soft glow
  Fade off at eventime,
As one who nursed a pleasant dream
  Of some delicious clime.

Thus, sweetly as the flowers that once
  She wore at eventide,
Faded and drooped the gentle girl,
  A blossom by our side,
And her young light of life went out
  With sunset, when she died !

THE CONVICT'S CHILD.

Unlock the still home of the dead;
Down to its slumber we would lay
One, who, with firm, unshrinking tread,
Drew near and nearer day by day.

For when the morn of life for her
Hid all its beautiful light in tears,
The shadow of the sepulchre
Woke in her soul no human fears.

Even in the spring-time of her youth,
Before that she had wept or striven,
With all its wealth of love and truth,
She gave her young heart up to heaven.

Something prophetic of her doom
  Before her vision sadly rose ;
So, ere the evil days had come,
  She gathered strength to meet their woes.

Child of a lost and guilty sire,
  She felt, what time must darkly prove,
That home and hearth were not for her,
  Nor the sweet ministries of love.

And when her trembling heart at last
  By maiden hopes and fears was thrilled,
Clasping the sacred cross more fast,
  That pleading for the earth was stilled.

Turning from eyes whose tender ray
  Burned with affection true and deep,
Love's passionate kisses never lay
  Upon her forehead but in sleep.

Yet more than mortal may be tried
  Was she who firmly bore that part,
And the meek martyr slowly died
  In crushing down the human heart.

Pitying in such a world of storms
 The woes of that unsheltered breast,
Death kindly took her in his arms,
 And rocked her to eternal rest.

Then softly, softly, down to sleep,
 Lay her where these white blossoms grow,
And where the Sabbath silence deep
 Is broken by no sound of woe; —

Where near her, the long summer through,
 Will sing this gently lulling stream;
'T is the first rest she ever knew,
 Haunted by no unquiet dream.

AT THE WATER'S EDGE.

THERE are little innocent ones,
  And their love is wondrous strong,
Clinging about her neck,
  But they may not keep her long.

Father! give her strength
  To loosen their grasp apart,
And to fold her empty hands
  Calmly over her heart.

And if the mists of doubt
  Fearfully rise and climb
Up from that river that rolls
  Close by the shore of time, —

Suddenly rend it away,
  Holy and Merciful One!
As the veil of the temple was rent,
  When the mission of Christ was done.

So she can see the clime
  Where the jasper walls begin,
And the pearl gates, half unclosed,
  Ready to shut her in.

So she can see the saints,
  As they beckon with shining hand,
Leaning over the towers,
  Waiting to see her land.

Saviour! we wait thy aid,
  For our human aid were vain;
We have gone to the water's edge,
  And must turn to the world again.

For she stands where the waves of death
  Fearfully surge and beat,
And the rock of the shore of life
  Is shelving under her feet.

DEAD.

DEAD! yet there comes no shriek, no tear,—
My agony is dumb;
I 've thought, and feared, and known so long
That such an hour must come:

For when her once sweet household cares
Grew wearier every day,
And, dropping from her listless hand,
Her work was put away,

I knew that all her tasks were done,
And, though I wept and prayed,
I always thought of her as one
For whom the shroud is made.

She talked of growing strong and well,
  To soothe our parting pain :
I knew it would be well with her
  Before we met again ; —

I knew upon that lonesome hill,
  Where winter now is drear,
They 'd have to make another grave
  Before another year.

I hope that they will dig it there :
  I would not have it made
Between the graves where strangers sleep,
  Under the cypress shade.

I 'd have it where our sisters gone
  Are sleeping side by side,
And where we weeping orphans laid
  Our mother when she died.

There, too, with beauty scarcely dimmed,
  And curls of shining gold,
We covered little Ellie's face,
  And hid it in the mould.

So bring her there, and when they rise
  Who in the dust have lain,
She 'll see her little baby wake,
  And take him up again.

THE WATCHER'S STORY.

SHE has slept since first the firelight
   Mingled with the sun's last ray, —
If she lives till after midnight
   She may see another day ; —
Though she then could only number
   A few weary hours, at best,
And 't were better if her slumber
   Could be deepened into rest.

When about my neck, all night through,
   White arms, softly dimpled, lay,
Then her face had not a shadow
   That I could not kiss away :

And I knew the simple measure
  Of her little hopes and fears,
Shared in all her childish pleasure,
  Pitied all her childish fears.
But the maiden's deeper yearning
  Taught her maidenhood's disguise,
When a tenderer light came burning
  In the soft depths of her eyes.
Then she wandered down the meadows,
  Like some restless woodland elf,
Or sat hidden deep in shadows,
  Singing softly to herself,
Or repeated dreams elysian
  From some poet's touching strain,
As some vague and nameless vision
  Were half-formed within the brain.
I had counselled, led, reproved her,—
  Now the time for these was o'er;
From a baby I had loved her,
  She could be a child no more.

Then she grew a listless weeper,
  Scarce her lip might lightly speak,
And the crimson glow was deeper
  In the white snow of her cheek.

And sometimes, at midnight waking,
  I have heard her bitter sighs,
And have seen the tear-drops breaking
  Through the closed lids of her eyes.
Sometimes, like a shaken blossom,
  Moved her heart with visions sweet;
With my hand upon her bosom,
  I could feel it beat, and beat.
While her young face down the meadows
  Kept in childhood's pleasant track,
I could kiss off all the shadows,
  Other lips had kissed them back!
Oftener then the tear-dews pearly
  Dropped upon her soft white cheek,
Sorrow came to her so early,
  And her womanhood was weak.
Life grew weary, very weary:
  I had trembled, knowing well
Evermore it must be dreary,
  When the first great shadow fell.
It had fallen, — the old, sad story,
  Hope deferred, and wearying doubt;
From her youth's first crown of glory
  All the roses had dropped out.

Once, when husbandmen were bearing
  To their barns the ripened ear,
And that sorrow had been wearing
  On her mortal life a year;
As she sat with me at evening,
  Looking earnestly without,
Still half hopeful, and half yielding
  To the bitterness of doubt;
Anxiously towards me leaning,
  Breaking off a lonesome tune,
She asked, with deepest meaning,
  If the year had worn to June.
Said I, roses lately blooming
  Have all faded from their prime;
And she answered, He is coming!
  'T is the season, 't is the time!

Then she looked adown the valley
  Towards the pleasant fields in sight,
Where the wheat was hanging heavy
  And the rye was growing white;
And she said, with full heart beating,
  And with earnest, trembling tone,
"If to-night should be our meeting,
  Let me see him first alone."

So with trust still unabated,
  With affection deep and true,
She watched, and hoped, and waited,
  All the lonesome summer through,
Till the autumn wind blew dreary ;
  Then she almost ceased to smile,
And her spirit grew more weary
  Of its burden all the while.
I remember well of sharing
  The last watch she ever kept,
Till she turned away despairing,
  Saying sadly while she wept: —

"Shut the window! when 't is lifted
  I can feel the cheerless rain,
And the yellow leaves are drifted
  O'er me, through the open pane.
Heavy shadows, creeping nigher,
  Darken over all the walk :
Let us sit beside the fire,
  Where we used to sit and talk.
Close the shutter, through the gloaming
  My poor eyes can see no more,
And if any one is coming
  I shall hear them at the door.

O my friend, but speak, and cheer me, —
  Speak until my heart grow light;
What if he were very near me, —
  What if he should come to night!
It might be so, — ere the morrow
  He might sit there where thou art,
And the weight of all this sorrow
  Be uplifted from my heart.
Idle, idle, long endurance
  Changes hope to fear and doubt,
Saying oft a sweet assurance
  Almost wears its meaning out.
O, my thoughts are foolish dreaming,
  Fancies of a troubled brain,
Very like the truth in seeming;
  But he will not come again.
Never will his hand caress me,
  Pushing back this faded hair,
Never whisper soft, 'God bless thee!'
  Half in fondness, half in prayer.
Well, if he were standing near me,
  Close as thou hast stood to-day,
Could I make the Father hear me,
  Could I turn from him to pray?

O my friend, whose soul was never
  On such waves of passion tost,
Plead for Heaven's sweet mercy ever,
  That I be not wholly lost!
Talk to me of peaceful bosoms,
  Never touched by mortal ills;
Talk of beds of fragrant blossoms,
  Whitening all the fadeless hills.
Promises of sweet Evangels,
  Blessed hope of life above,
O eternity, O angels!
  Turn my thoughts from human love!"

RESOLVES.

I HAVE said I would not meet him ;
  Have I said the words in vain ?
Sunset burns along the hill-tops,
  And I 'm waiting here again.
But my promise is not broken,
  Though I stand where once we met ;
When I hear his coming footsteps,
  I can fly him even yet.

We have stood here oft, when evening
  Deepened slowly o'er the plain ;
But I must not, dare not, meet him
  In the shadows here again ;

For I could not turn away and leave
  That pleading look and tone,
And the sorrow of his parting
  Would be bitter as my own.

In the dim and distant ether
  The first star is shining through,
And another and another
  Tremble softly in the blue:
Should I linger but one moment
  In the shadows where I stand,
I shall see the vine-leaves parted,
  With a quick, impatient hand.

But I will not wait his coming!
  He will surely come once more;
Though I said I would not meet him,
  I have told him so before;
And he knows the stars of evening
  See me standing here again, —
O, he surely will not leave me
  Now to watch and wait in vain!

'T is the hour, the time of meeting!
  In one moment 't will be past;

And last night he stood beside me, —
  Was that blessed time the last?
I could better bear my sorrow,
  Could I live that parting o'er;
O, I wish I had not told him
  That I would not come *once* more!

Could that have been the night-wind
  Moved the branches thus apart?
Did I hear a coming footstep,
  Or the beating of my heart?
No! I hear him, I can see him,
  And my weak resolves are vain;
I will fly, — but to his bosom,
  And to leave it not again!

DREAMS.

Whate'er before my sight appears,
One vision in my heart is borne, —
Two sweet, sad faces, wet with tears,
Seen through the dim, gray light of morn.

And, half o'ershadowing them, arise
Thoughts, which are never lulled to sleep,
Of one, whose calm, rebuking eyes
Are sadder that they do not weep.

O friend, whose lot it might not be
To tread, with me, life's path of ills!
O friend, who yet shalt walk with me
The white path of the eternal hills!

Gone are the moments when we planned
  Those sweet, but unsubstantial bowers,
In some unknown and pleasant land,
  Where all our future wound through flowers.

Into the past eternity
  Have faded all those hopes and schemes;
That summer island in the sea
  Slept only in our sea of dreams.

I know not if our hope was sin,
  When that fair structure was upbuilt;
But this I know, that mine has been
  The bitterest recompense of guilt.

And the wild tempest of despair
  Still sweeps my spirit like a blast;
Tears, penance, agonizing prayer,—
  Could you not save me from the past!

PROPHECIES.

An urn within her claspèd hands,
Brimful and running o'er with dew,
Spring on the green hills smiling stands,
Or walks in pleasant valley-lands,
Through sprouting grass and violets blue.
And but this morn, almost before
The sunshine came its leaves to gild,
In the old elm that shades our door,
There came a timid bird to build.

O time of flowers! O time of song!
How does my heart rejoice again!
For pleasant things to thee belong;
And desolate, and drear, and long,
To me was Winter's lonesome reign:

Since last thou trodd'st the vale and hill,
  And nature with delight was rife,
A shadow strange, and dark, and chill,
  Has hung above my house of life.

But now I see its blackness drift
  Away, away, from out my sky;
And, as its heavy folds uplift,
There shines upon me, through the rift,
  A burning star of prophecy:
My heart is singing with the birds,
  Life's orb has passed from its eclipse;
And some sweet poet's hopeful words
  Are always, always, on my lips.

O thou who lov'st me! O my friend!
  Whate'er thy fears, where'er thou art,
As these soft skies above thee bend,
Does not their pleasant sunshine lend
  A gleam of sunshine to thy heart?
Sweet prophecies through all the day
  Within my bosom softly thrill,
And, while the night-time wears away,
  My sleep with pleasant visions fill.

And I must whisper unto thee,
  Thou, who hast waited long in vain;
Though distant still the day may be,
It shall be in our destiny
  To tread the selfsame path again;
And over hills, with blossoms white,
  Or lingering by the singing streams,
That path shall wander on in light,
  And life be happier than our dreams!

THE CONFESSION.

In the moonlight of the Spring-time,
  Trembling, blushing, half afraid,
Heard I first the fond confession
  From the sweet lips of the maid.

As the roses of the Summer,
  By his warm embraces won,
Take a fairer, richer color
  From the glances of the sun ; —

So as, gazing, earnest, anxious,
  I besought her but to speak,
Deep and deeper burned the crimson
  Of the blushes in her cheek ; —

Till at last, with happy impulse,
  Impulse that she might not check,
As it softly thrilled and trembled,
  Stole her white arm round my neck : —

And with lips, that, half averted
  From the lips that bent above,
Met the kiss of our betrothal,
  Told the maiden of her love.

THE POEM.

I am dreaming o'er a poem
  Of affection's strength sublime;
Loved, because that once I read it
  In the dear, dear olden time,
While you sat and praised my reading
  Of the poet's touching rhyme.

And how often, very gently,
  Did you check my cadence, when
I read the sweetest verses
  Over to you once again!
I have read that blessed poem
  Many, many times since then!

Then you softly closed the volume,
  When I paused at the last line,
While your eyes said sweeter poems, —
  Poems that were more divine ;
And all Hybla sweets were clustered
  On the lips that dropped to mine.

This is over now, all over, —
  And 't is better thus to be ;
Yet I often sit and wonder
  Who is reading soft to thee,
And if any voice is sweeter
  To thy heart than mine would be !

TO ONE WHO SANG OF LOVE.

THOU hast sung of love's confession
  Out beneath the starry skies,
Of the rapture of the moment
  When the soul is breathed in sighs,
And the maiden's trembling transport
  As she blushingly replies
To the worship of a lover,
  Breathed from speaking lips and eyes.

By the earnest, tender pathos
  Of thy every witching line,
Such an hour of bliss ecstatic
  Has surely once been thine :

And I would that Heaven might answer
  This earnest wish of mine,
That thy star of love and beauty
  May wane not, nor decline.

Listening to the first confession,
  Lingering o'er the first fond kiss, —
What an age of bliss is crowded
  In an hour of life like this!
Surely thine at such a moment
  Has been perfect happiness,
And the maiden, the fond maiden,
  O, I cannot guess her bliss!

Sometimes to my heart in slumber
  Thought so like the truth will steal,
That the pressure of sweet kisses
  On my brow I almost feel;
And I dream fond lips have uttered
  What they might no more conceal;
But I cannot, no, I cannot,
  Make such blessed visions real.

ARCHIE.

O to be back in the beautiful shadow
Of that old maple-tree down in the meadow,
Watching the smiles that grew dearer and dearer,
Listening to lips that drew nearer and nearer!
O to be back in the crimson-topped clover,
Sitting again with my Archie, my lover!

O for the time when I felt his caresses
Smoothing away from my forehead the tresses,
When up from my heart to my cheek went the blushes,
As he said that my voice was as sweet as the thrush's, —
When he said that my eyes were bewitchingly jetty,
And I told him 't was only my love made them pretty.

Talk not of maiden reserve and of duty,
Or hide from my vision such wonderful beauty;
Pulses above may beat calmly and even, —
We have been fashioned for earth, and not heaven;
Angels are perfect, — I am but a woman;
Saints may be passionless, — Archie is human.

Talk not of heavenly, down-dropping blisses, —
Can they fall on the brow like the rain of soft kisses?
Preach not the promise of priests and evangels, —
Love-crowned, I ask not the crown of the angels;
All that the wall of pure jasper incloses
Makes not less lovely the white bridal roses.

Tell me, that, when all this life shall be over,
I shall still love him, and he be my lover, —
That in meadows far sweeter than clover or heather
My Archie and I shall sit always together,
Loving eternally, wed ne'er to sever, —
Then you may tell me of heaven for ever!

MAIDEN FEARS.

He knows that I love him ;
O, how could he tell
What I thought I would keep
In my bosom so well,
By guarding each action,
Each word, I might say !
Yet he knows that I love him, —
O, woe to the day !

To hide it I tried
By each innocent art,
And I thought I had kept it
Down deep in my heart :

Yet vain was my effort,
  My pride through the past,
Since my weakness, my folly,
  Have shown it at last.

'T was last night that he learned it,
  When down in the grove
He whispered me something
  Of hope and of love ;
'T was not that I faltered,
  I dared not to speak, —
But the blood mounted up
  From my heart to my cheek.

Not mine was the fault
  That such weakness was shown, —
O, he should not have kissed me
  By starlight alone !
And I thought, till I saw
  How he guessed at my love,
I thought that the shadows
  Were deeper above !

Nay, thou canst not console me,
  My hopes are undone ;

He will say that too lightly
  My heart has been won ;
And this spot on my forehead
  For ever will burn,
For he knows that I love him, —
  He will not return !

He will say 't was unmaidly
  Thus to reveal
What I might not, I could not,
  That moment conceal ;
And the heart he has won
  Will cast lightly aside ; —
O, I would, ere he knew it,
  I would I had died !

O thou who hast never
  Been faithless to me,
Crushed, bleeding, and broken,
  My heart turns to thee :
Friend, counsellor, sister,
  Through all things the same,
Let me hide in thy bosom
  My blushes of shame !

THE UNGUARDED MOMENT.

Yes, my lips to-night have spoken
  Words I said they should not speak;
And I would I could recall them, —
  Would I had not been so weak.
O that one unguarded moment!
  Were it mine to live again,
All the strength of its temptation
  Would appeal to me in vain.

True, my lips have only uttered
  What is ever in my heart:
I am happy when beside him,
  Wretched when we are apart;

Though I listen to his praises,
  Always longer than I should,
Yet my heart can never hear them
  Half so often as it would!

And I would not, could not, pain him,
  Would not for the world offend, —
I would have him know I like him,
  As a brother, as a friend;
But I meant to keep one secret
  In my bosom always hid,
For I never meant to tell him
  That I loved him, — but I did.

NELLY.

I 'M glad you " don't love him,"
  I really did fear
(Nay, frown not so terribly,
  Nelly, my dear);
His voice was so witching,
  His eyes were so bright,
Though you did not yet love him,
  I feared that you might!

So you 're candid, now, Nelly,
  You 're telling me true,
" His voice never sounded
  Bewitching to you."

Yet I sometimes have thought,
  When you heard his soft tone,
That a little more tenderness
  Spoke in your own.

And you 're sure you don't care, now,
  My dear little elf,
" Who else he talks love to,
  So 't is not yourself."
Sometimes when your forehead
  Such crimson would take,
I suspected — no matter,
  I 've made a mistake.

Nay, do not now, Nelly,
  O, do not be mad!
Since you say you don't love him,
  It makes me so glad;
Because I would never
  Have told it, you see,
But honestly, darling,
  He 's talked love to me!

Are you glad he has done
  What you wished him to do, —

That he talked about love
  To another than you ?
Yes, you surely must feel
  Quite a sense of relief ; —
But those tears are not joyous,
  That sob is like grief !

He said he had hidden it
  Long in his breast ; —
How you tremble ! — nay, listen,
  I 'll tell you the rest.
He said, just as true
  As I sit here alive,
That he loved you dear Nelly, —
  Aha ! you revive !

BURNING THE LETTERS.

I SAID that they were valueless, —
  I 'd rather have them not, —
All that since made them precious
  Was, or should have been, forgot;
I would do it very willingly,
  And not because I ought, —
But I did not, somehow, find it
  Quite so easy as I thought.

One was full of pleasant flattery, —
  I do not think I 'm vain,
And yet I paused a moment
  To read it once again.

One repeated dear, old phrases
  I had heard a thousand times;
I had read him once some verses,
  And another praised my rhymes.

One was just exactly like him, —
  Such a pretty little note!
One was interspersed with poetry
  That lovers always quote.
I don't know why I read them,
  Unless 't was just to know,
Since they once had been so precious,
  What had ever made them so.

I had told him when we parted
  To think no more of me;
And I 'm sure he 's nothing to me, —
  Indeed, why should he be?
Yet the flame sunk down to ashes,
  And I sat and held them still;
But I said that I would burn them, —
  And, some other time, I will!

A LAMENT.

ONCE in the season of childhood's joy,
  Dreaming never of life's great ills,
Hand in hand with a happy boy,
  I walked about on my native hills, —

Gathering berries ripe and fair,
  Pressing them oft to his smiling lip,
Braiding flowers in his sunny hair,
  And letting the curls through my fingers slip, —

Watching the clouds of the evening pass
  Over the moon in her home of blue;
Or chasing fireflies over the grass,
  Till our feet were wet with the summer dew.

Now I walk on the hills alone,
  Dreaming never of hope or joy,
And over a dungeon's floor of stone
  Sweep the curls of that happy boy.

And every night when a rose-hedge springs
  Up from the ashes of sunset's pyre,
And the eve-star, folding her golden wings,
  Drops like a bird in the leaves of fire, —

I sit and think how he entered in,
  And farther and farther, every time,
Followed the downward way of sin,
  Till it led to the awful gates of crime.

I sit and think, till my great despair
  Rises up like a mighty wave,
How fast the locks of my father's hair
  Are whitening now for the quiet grave.

But never reproach on my lip has been,
  Never one moment can I forget,
Though bound in prison and lost in sin,
  My brother once is my brother yet.

THE LULLABY.

THROUGH the open summer lattice,
  Half revealed and half in shade,
Yesternight I saw a mortal
  Whose remembrance will not fade.

Little birds their heads had hidden
  Under wings of gold and brown;
Lily bells and luscious blossoms
  Softly had been folded down;

Fountains, with their quiet dropping,
  Only lulled the drowsy bees;
And the wind was lightly going
  In and out the tops of trees;

But that pale and restless creature —
Had she dreamed too much before? —
Seemed as one whom sleep would visit
Never, never, never more.

Rocking by the summer lattice,
Rocking to and fro, she sung,
O, the saddest, saddest music
Ever fell from mortal tongue!

So she strove to hush the crying,
Bitterer that 't was faint and low,
Of the little baby pressing
Close against her heart of woe.

And her words were very mournful,
And so very, very faint;
She was keeping down her anguish,
That no ear might hear her plaint.

"Lullaby, my wretched baby;
Go to sleep, and sleep till morn!
Lullaby, my wretched baby;
Would that thou hadst not been born!

"Mock me not with open eyelids,
  For thine eyes are soft and blue;
While in mine the midnight blackness
  Deepens, looking down on you.

"Time shall bind about your forehead
  Sunny hair in golden bands;
Tangle not my raven tresses
  With your soft and clinging hands!

"Lullaby, my wretched baby:
  O, how long the watches seem!
Lullaby, my wretched baby;
  Dream and smile, and smile and dream!

"O the sad eyes of my mother!
  O my brother, proud and brave!
O the white hair of my father,
  Drooping sadly toward the grave!

"O my sister, pure as heaven,
  Here thy head in sleep has lain!
Never on this wretched bosom
  Canst thou pillow it again!

" Lullaby, my wretched baby ;
  Live I only for thy sake !
Lullaby, my wretched baby ;
  Sleep, and dream, and never wake ! "

LEFT ALONE.

She 's left me here alone again:
  'T will be a weary lot,
Through all this cheerless winter time
  To live where she is not;
To sit, where once we used to sit,
  With smileless lip and dumb;
To count the moments since she went,
  And know not when she 'll come!

We talked through all the summer time,
  We 'd talked through all the spring,
Of how about the winter hearth
  We 'd make a pleasant ring;

Of how with loving words and looks
  The time should all be sped ; —
The firelight's glow is mournful now,
  The books are all unread.

We never were together long,
  We have not been so blest ;
I might have known this hope of ours
  Would perish like the rest :
And half I trembled all the while,
  And feared it would be so ; —
The hand of fate would press me back
  From where her feet must go.

If there shall ever be a time,
  When, as in days that were,
My soul can whisper all its dreams
  And all its thoughts to her, —
When I can share her heart's sweet hopes,
  Or soothe its bitter pain, —
I would the hours were past till then,
  And that were come again !

THE RETROSPECT.

As one who sees life's hopes have end,
  And cannot hush the bitter cry,
Thou weep'st for that lost vale, my friend,
  Where childhood's pleasant places lie;
And looking down the sloping track
  Where now our lonesome steps are told,
Wouldst softly roll the seasons back,
  And leave us children as of old.

Nay, weave sweet fancies as you will,
  Yet what is childish happiness
To such great rapture as can fill
  The heart of womanhood with bliss?

And though the trials which years must bring
  Have come, and left thee what thou art,
Think what a great and wondrous thing
  Is victory o'er the human heart!

Life's sparkling wine for us is dim,
  Only the bitter drops remain;
Yet, for the brightness on the brim,
  Who would not drink the draught of pain?
And not in even ways, my friend,
  Attains the soul to regions higher;
If step by step our feet ascend,
  Their path must be a path of fire!

ONE SHALL BE TAKEN.

DEAR friend, whose presence always made
Even the dreariest night-time glad, —
Whose lengthening absence darkens o'er
The little sunshine that I had, —
My heart is sad for thee to-night,
And every wretched thought of mine
Reaches across the lonesome hills,
That lie between my home and thine.

O woods, wherein our childish feet,
Gathering the summer blossoms, strayed !
O meadows, white with clover-blooms !
O soft, green hollows, where we played !

Can you not cool that aching brow,
  With all your shadows and your dew ;
And charm the slow and languid step
  Back to the joyous life it knew ?

Most loved, most cherished, since that hour
  When, as she blest thee o'er and o'er,
Our mother put thee from her arms,
  To feel thy kisses never more ;
And I, that scarce were missed, am spared,
  While o'er thy way the shadow lies, —
Infinite Mercy surely knew
  Thou wert the fittest for the skies !

THE BROTHERS.

We had no home, we only had
A shelter for our head:
How poor we were, how scantily
We all were clothed and fed!
But though a wretched little child,
I know not why or how,
I did not feel it half so much
As I can feel it now!

When mother sat at night and sewed,
My rest was calm and deep;
I did not know that she was tired,
Or that she needed sleep.

She wrapped the covering round our bed,
  In many an ample fold ;
She had not half so much herself
  To keep her from the cold.

I know it now, I know it all, —
  They knew it then above, —
Her life of patient sacrifice,
  And never-tiring love.
I know, for then her tasks seemed done, —
  We all were grown beside, —
How glad she must have been to go,
  After the baby died !

I do not care to deck me now
  With costly robe or gaud, —
My mother dressed so plain at home,
  And never went abroad.
I do not even want a shroud
  Of linen, white and pure, —
They made our little baby one
  That was so coarse and poor.

I had another brother then,
  I prayed that God would save ;

I knew not life had darker dooms
   Than lying in the grave.
I did not know, when o'er the dead
   So bitterly I cried,
I 'd live to wish a thousand times
   The other, too, had died.

REMORSE.

O sweetest friend I ever had,
How sinks my heavy heart to know
That life, which was so bright for thee,
Has lost its sunshine and its glow !

I cannot think of thee as one
Sighing for calm repose in vain ;
Nor of the beauty of thy smile,
Faded and sadly dim with pain.

Thou surely shouldst not be to-day
Lying upon the autumn leaves,
But in the border-fields of hope,
Binding the blossoms into sheaves.

For, with a shadow on thy way,
  The sunshine of my life is o'er,
And flowery dell and fresh green holt
  Can charm my footsteps nevermore!

And if I have not always seen
  The beauty of thy deeds aright,—
If I have failed to make thy path
  As smooth and even as I might,—

Not thine the fault, but mine the sin,
  And I have felt its heaviest curse
Fall on the heart that aches to-day,
  With vain repentance and remorse,—

A heart that lifts its cry to thee,
  Above this wild and awful blast,
That, sweeping from the hills of home,
  Brings bitterest memories of the past.

O, sweet forgiveness, from thy love,
  Send to me o'er the waste between;
Not as thou hop'st to be forgiven,
  For thou hast never bowed to sin.

Pure as thy light of life was given,
  Thou still hast kept its steady flame;
And the chaste garment of thy soul
  Is white and spotless as it came.

PROPHECY.

No great sea lifts its angry waves
  Between me and the friend most dear,
And over all our household graves
  The grass has grown for many a year.

With all that makes the heart rejoice,
  The days of summer go and come;
No feeble step, no failing voice,
  Saddens the chambers of our home.

Yet, though I know, and feel, and see,
  God's blessings all about my way,
The burden of sad prophecy
  Lies heavy on my soul to-day.

These awful words of destiny
  Are sounding in my heart and brain :
" Not an unbroken family
  Shall summer find us here again ! "

O God ! if this indeed be so,
  Whose pillow then shall be unprest ?
Whose heart, that feels life's pleasant glow,
  Shall faint, and beat itself to rest ?

Eternal silence makes reply,
  We may not, cannot know our doom ;
No voice comes downward from the sky,
  No voice comes upward from the tomb.

Yet this I would not ask in vain :
  Hide from my wretched eyes the day
When by our household graves again
  The turf is lightly put away !

First from our home, though all descend
  At last to that one place of rest,
O solemn Earth ! O mighty Friend !
  Take me and hide me in thy breast !

THE DREAMER.

Blow life's most fearful tempest, blow,
  And make the midnight wild and rough;
My soul shall battle with you now, —
  I 've been a dreamer long enough!

Open, O sea, a darker path,
  Dash to my lips the angry spray;
The tenth wave of thy fiercest wrath
  Were nothing to my strength to-day!

Though floating onward listlessly
  When pleasant breezes softly blew,
My spirit with the adverse sea
  Shall rise, and gather strength anew.

Wake, soul of mine, and be thou strong;
Keep down thy weakness, human heart;
Thou hast unnerved my arm too long,
O foolish dreamer that thou art!

For I have sat and mused for hours
Of havens that I yet should see,
Of winding paths of pleasant flowers,
And summer islands in the sea, —

Forgetful of the storms that come,
Of winds that dig the ocean grave,
And sharp reefs hidden by the foam
That drifts like blossoms on the wave, —

Forgetful, too, that he who guides
Must have a firm and steadfast hand,
If e'er his vessel safely rides
Through storm and breaker to the land, —

Idly and listless drifting on,
Feeding my fancy all the while,
As lovesick dreamers feed upon
The honeyed sweetness of a smile.

Fool that I was, — ay ! Folly's mock, —
  To think not, in those pleasant hours,
How barks have foundered on the rock,
  And drifted past the isles of flowers !

Yet well it were, if, roused to feel,
  I yet avert such fearful fate, —
The quick, sharp grating of the keel
  Had been a warning all too late.

But courage still ; for whether now
  Or rough or smooth life's ocean seems,
To-day my soul records her vow,
  Hereafter I am done with dreams !

THE CONSECRATION.

O SOUL, that must survive that hour
  When heart shall fail and flesh decay !
God, angels, men, are witnesses
  Of vows which thou hast made to-day.
What solemn fears this hour are born,
  What joyful hopes this hour are given !
Thought reaches down from heaven to hell,
  And up from farthest hell to heaven.

Before my fearful vision pass
  Those star-like souls, grown darkly dim, —
The sea of mingled glass and fire,
  The saints and priests with conquering hymn.

O God! shall I go down with those,
  Wandering through blackness from their place,
Or up with the redeemed and saved,
  Who stand before their Father's face?

For now my eyes have seen the truth,
  This is thy sure and just decree:
"If I shall turn again to sin,
  There is no sacrifice for me":
And the baptismal touch, which lay
  So lightly on the brow beneath,
Shall be omnipotent in power,
  To press me surely down to death.

Its seal shall be a diadem,
  To shine amid the angel choir,
Or on my forehead burn in hell,
  An everlasting crown of fire;
And all who hear my vows to-day
  Shall hear my final sentence read:
God, angels, men, are witnesses
  At the great judgment of the dead.

DRAWING WATER.

I HAD drunk, with lip unsated,
Where the founts of pleasure burst;
I had hewn out broken cisterns,
And they mocked my spirit's thirst:

And I said, life is a desert,
Hot, and measureless, and dry;
And God will not give me water,
Though I pray, and faint, and die.

Spoke there then a friend and brother,
"Rise, and roll the stone away;
There are founts of life upspringing
In thy pathway every day."

Then I said my heart was sinful,
  Very sinful was my speech ;
All the wells of God's salvation
  Are too deep for me to reach.

And he answered, " Rise and labor, —
  Doubt and idleness is death ;
Shape thee out a goodly vessel
  With the strong hands of thy faith."

So I wrought and shaped the vessel,
  Then knelt lowly, humbly there,
And I drew up living water
  With the golden chain of prayer.

SOLEMNITY OF LIFE.

WHETHER are cast our destinies
  In peaceful ways, or ways of strife ;
A solemn thing to us it is,
  This mystery of human life.

Solemn, when first, unconscious, dumb,
  Within an untried world we stand,
Immortal beings that have come
  Newly from God's creating hand.

And solemn, even as 'tis fleet,
  The time when, learning childish fears,
We cross, with scarcely balanced feet,
  The threshold of our mortal years.

'T is solemn, when, with parting smiles,
  We leave its innocence and truth,
To learn how deeper than the child's
  Are all the loves and fears of youth.

It is a solemn thing to snap
  The cords of human love apart;
More solemn still to feel them wrap
  Their wondrous strength about the heart.

'T is solemn to have ever known
  The pleadings of the soul unmoved, —
Solemn to feel ourselves alone;
  More solemn still to be beloved.

It is a solemn thing to wear
  The roses of the bridal wreath, —
Solemn the words we utter there,
  Of faith unchanging until death.

Solemn is life, when God unlocks
  The fountain in the soul most deep, —
Solemn the heart-beat, when it rocks
  A young immortal to its sleep.

'T is solemn when the Power above
  Darkens our being's living spark,—
Solemn to see the friends we love
  Going downward from us to the dark.

O human life, when all thy woes
  And all thy trials are struggled through,
What can eternity disclose
  More wondrous solemn than we knew!

MY BLESSINGS.

GREAT waves of plenty rolling up
  Their golden billows to our feet,
Fields where the ungathered rye is white,
  Or heavy with the yellow wheat; —

Wealth surging inward from the sea,
  And plenty through our land abroad,
With sunshine resting over all,
  That everlasting smile of God!

For these, yet not for these alone,
  My tongue its gratitude would say:
All the great blessings of my life
  Are present in my thought to-day.

For more than all my mortal wants
  Have been, O God, thy full supplies ;—
Health, shelter, and my daily bread,
  For these my grateful thanks arise.

For ties of faith, whose wondrous strength
  Time nor eternity can part;
For all the words of love that fall
  Like living waters on my heart;

For even that fearful strife, where sin
  Was conquered and subdued at length,
Temptations met and overcome,
  Whereby my soul has gathered strength ;

For all the warnings that have come
  From mortal agony or death;
For even that bitterest storm of life,
  Which drove me on the rock of faith.

For all the past I thank thee, God!
  And for the future trust in thee,
Whate'er of trial or blessing yet,
  Asked or unasked, thou hast for me.

Yet only this one boon I crave, —
  After life's brief and fleeting hour,
Make my belovéd thy beloved,
  And keep us in thy day of power!

SABBATH THOUGHTS.

I AM sitting all the while
Looking down the solemn aisle,
Toward the saints and martyrs old,
Standing in their niches cold, —
Toward the wings of cherubs fair,
Veiling half their golden hair,
And the painted light that falls
Through the window on the walls.

I can see the revered flow
Of soft garments, white as snow,
And the shade of silver hair
Dropping on the book of prayer.

I can hear the litany,
"Miserable sinners, we!"
And the organ swelling higher,
And the chanting of the choir.

And I marvel if with them,
In the New Jerusalem,
I shall hear the sacred choir
Chant with flaming tongues of fire;
If I e'er shall find a place
With the ransomed, saved by grace;
If my feet shall ever tread
Where the just are perfected?

Not, my soul, as now thou art;
Not with this rebellious heart;
Not with nature unsubdued,
Evil overshadowing good;
Not while I for pardon seek
With a faith so faint and weak;
Not while tempted thus to sin,
From without and from within!

Thou whom love did once compel
Down from heaven to sleep in hell;

Thou whose mercy purged from dross
Even the thief upon the cross,
Save me, O thou bleeding Lamb,
Chief of sinners though I am,
When, with clouds about thee furled,
Thou shalt come to judge the world!

NEARER HOME.

ONE sweetly solemn thought
  Comes to me o'er and o'er, —
I am nearer home to-day
  Than I have ever been before ; —

Nearer my Father's house
  Where the many mansions be ;
Nearer the great white throne,
  Nearer the jasper sea ; —

Nearer the bound of life
  Where we lay our burdens down ;
Nearer leaving the cross,
  Nearer gaining the crown.

But lying darkly between,
 Winding down through the night,
Is the dim and unknown stream
 That leads at last to the light.

Closer and closer my steps
 Come to the dark abysm ;
Closer death to my lips
 Presses the awful chrysm.

Father, perfect my trust ;
 Strengthen the might of my faith ;
Let me feel as I would when I stand
 On the rock of the shore of death, —

Feel as I would when my feet
 Are slipping o'er the brink ;
For it may be I 'm nearer home, —
 Nearer now than I think.

HYMN.

God of the Sabbath, calm and still,
  Father, in whom we live and move,
How do our trembling bosoms thrill
  With words which tell us of thy love !

Thine heralds, speaking of the tomb,
  The organ's voice, the censer's flame,
The solemn minster's shadowy gloom,
  Awe us, and make us fear thy name.

The earthquake, opening deep its graves,
  The lightning, running down the sky,
The great sea, lifting up its waves,
  Speak of thine awful majesty !

But once thou camest in Eden's prime,
  Lord of the soul, to talk with men,
And in the cool of eventime
  Thou seemest with us, now as then.

For when our trembling souls draw near,
  And silence keeps the earth and sea,
Thou speak'st, with no interpreter
  To stand between our hearts and thee!

SOWING SEED.

Go and sow beside all waters,
In the morning of thy youth,
In the evening scatter broadcast
Precious seeds of living truth.

For though much may sink and perish
In the rocky, barren mould,
And the harvest of thy labor
May be less than thirty-fold,

Let thy hand be not withholden,
Still beside all waters sow,
For thou know'st not which shall prosper,
Whether this or that will grow,

While some precious portion, scattered,
  Germinating, taking root,
Shall spring up, and grow, and ripen
  Into never-dying fruit.

Therefore, sow beside all waters,
  Trusting, hoping, toiling on;
When the fields are white for harvest,
  God will send his angels down.

And thy soul may see the value
  Of its patient morns and eves,
When the everlasting garner
  Shall be filled with precious sheaves.

THE BAPTISM.

From the waters of affliction,
From her baptism of dark woe,
With her sweet eyes very mournful,
And her forehead like the snow,

Came she up ; and, O, how many
In such hours of trial are seen,
When they faint with mortal weakness,
Knowing not whereon to lean !

With her face upon my bosom,
Said she then in accent sad,
As she wound her arms about me,
I was all the friend she had.

And I told her — pushing backward
  From her forehead like the snow,
All her tear-wet tresses, dripping
  With that baptism of dark woe —

How, in all that great affliction,
  Loving hands had led her on,
When she came up from the waters,
  Led her when her feet went down, —

And that only the good Father,
  He who thus her faith had tried,
Could have brought her through the billows,
  Safely to the other side.

And I told her how life's pilgrims
  Crossed that solemn stream beneath,
To a brighter pathway leading,
  Up the living hills of faith.

Lifting upward from my bosom
  Then her forehead like the snow,
I will weep, she said, no longer,
  Therefore rise and let us go!

And, as one who walks untroubled
  By no mortal doubt or fear,
Oft we heard her far above us,
  Singing hymns of lofty cheer, —

Till with feet that firmly balanced
  On faith's summit-rock she trod,
And beheld the shining bastions
  Of the city of our God.

Then her voice was tenderer, holier,
  She grew gentler all the while;
It was like a benediction
  But to see her patient smile.

As she walked with cheerful spirit
  Where her daily duties led,
"Father, keep me from temptation,"
  Was the only prayer she said.

Often made she earnest pleading,
  As she went from us apart,
To be saved through all her lifetime
  From the weakness of her heart.

And she prayed that she might never,
Never in her trials below,
Bring her soul before the altar,
Wailing in unchastened woe.

So her hands of faith were strengthened,
And when clouds about her lay,
From her bosom all the darkness
She could softly put away.

Smilingly she went unaided,
When we would have led her on,
Saying always to our pleading,
Better that I go alone.

Turned she from the faces dearest
When her feet more feebly trod,
That she might not then be tempted
By a mortal love from God.

So the Father, for her pleading,
Kept her safe through all life's hours,
And her path went brightly upward
To eternity through flowers.

THE CHRISTIAN WOMAN.

O, BEAUTIFUL as Morning in those hours
When, as her pathway lies along the hills,
Her golden fingers wake the dewy flowers,
And softly touch the waters of the rills,
Was she who walked more faintly day by day,
Till silently she perished by the way.

It was not hers to know that perfect heaven
Of passionate love returned by love as deep,
Not hers to sing the cradle-song at even,
Watching the beauty of her babe asleep;
"Mother and brethren," — these she had not known,
Save such as do the Father's will alone.

Yet found she something still for which to live, —
  Hearths desolate, where angel-like she came ;
And " little ones," to whom her hand could give
  A cup of water in her Master's name ;
And breaking hearts, to bind away from death
With the soft hand of pitying love and faith.

She never won the voice of popular praise,
  But, counting earthly triumph as but dross,
Seeking to keep her Saviour's perfect ways,
  Bearing in quiet paths his blessed cross,
She made her life, while with us here she trod,
A consecration to the will of God.

And she hath lived and labored not in vain :
  Through the deep prison-cells her accents thrill,
And the sad slave leans idly on his chain,
  And hears the music of her singing still ;
While little children, with their innocent praise,
Keep freshly in men's hearts her Christian ways.

And what a beautiful lesson she made known !
  The whiteness of her soul sin could not dim ;
Ready to lay down on God's altar-stone
  The dearest treasure of her life for Him,

Her flame of sacrifice never, never waned;
How could she live and die so self-sustained?

For friends supported not her parting soul,
  And whispered words of comfort, kind and sweet,
When treading onward to that final goal,
  Where the still Bridegroom waited for her feet;
Alone she walked, yet with a fearless tread,
Down to Death's chamber and his bridal bed!

THE HOSTS OF THOUGHT.

How heavy fall the evening shades,
  Making the earth more dark and drear,
As to its sunset sadly fades
  This, the last Sabbath of the year!

Oft, when the light has softly burned
  Among the clouds, as day was done,
I 've watched their golden furrows turned
  By the red ploughshare of the sun.

To-night, no track of billowy gold
  Is softly slanting down the skies;
But dull-gray bastions, dark and cold,
  Shut all the glory from my eyes.

And in the plain that lies below,
  What cheerless prospect meets my eye!
One long and level reach of snow,
  Stretching to meet the western sky!

While far across these lonesome vales,
  Like a lost soul, and unconfined,
Down through the mountain gorges wails
  The awful spirit of the wind.

When, yester-eve, the twilight stilled,
  With soft, caressing hand, the day,
Upon my heart, that joyous thrilled,
  A sweet, tumultuous vision lay.

To-night, in sorrow's arms enwound,
  I think of broken faith and trust,
And tresses, from their flowers unbound,
  Hid in the dimness of the dust.

And hopes that took their heavenward flight,
  As fancy lately gave them birth,
Slow through the solemn air to-night
  Are beating backward to the earth.

O memory, if the shadowy hand
Lock all thy death-crypts close and fast,
Call not my spirit back to stand
In the dark chamber of the past!

For trembling fear, and mortal doubt,
About me all day long have been;
So even the dreary world without
Is brighter than the world within.

Pale hosts of thought before me start:
O for that needed power I lack,
To guard the fortress of my heart,
And press their awful columns back!

O for a soul to meet their gaze,
And grapple fearless with its woe!
As the wild *athlete*, of old days,
In the embraces of the foe!

Thoughts of the many lost and loved, —
Each unfulfilled and noble plan, —
Memories of Sabbaths unimproved, —
Duty undone to God or man; —

They come, with solemn, warning frown,
  Like ghosts about some haunted tent;
And courage silently goes down,
  Before their dreadful armament.

O friend of mine, in years agone,
  Where'er, at this dark hour, thou art,
Why hast thou left me here alone,
  To fight the battles of the heart?

Alone? A soft eye's tender light
  Is turned to meet my anxious glance;
And, struggling upward from the night,
  My soul has broken from her trance.

Love is omnipotent to check
  Such 'wildering fancies of the brain;
A soft hand trembles on my neck,
  And lo, I sit with hope again!

Even the sky no longer seems
  Like a dull barrier, built afar;
And through its crumbling wall there gleams
  The sweet flame of one burning star.

The winds, that from the mountain's brow
  Came down the dreary plains to sweep,
Back, in the cavernous hollow, now
  Have softly sung themselves to sleep.

Come, thou, whose love no waning knows,
  And put thy gentle hand in mine,
For strong in faith my spirit grows,
  Leaning confidingly on thine.

And in the calm, or in the strife,
  If side by side with thee I move,
Hereafter I will live a life
  That shall not shame thy trusting love.

Memory and fear, with all their powers,
  No more my soul shall crush or bend ;
For the great future still is ours,
  And thou art with me, O my friend !

OUR HOMESTEAD.

Our old brown homestead reared its walls,
From the way-side dust aloof,
Where the apple-boughs could almost cast
Their fruitage on its roof:
And the cherry-tree so near it grew,
That when awake I 've lain,
In the lonesome nights, I 've heard the limbs,
As they creaked against the pane:
And those orchard trees, O those orchard trees!
I 've seen my little brothers rocked
In their tops by the summer breeze.

The sweet-brier under the window-sill,
Which the early birds made glad,

And the damask rose by the garden fence,
Were all the flowers we had.
I 've looked at many a flower since then,
Exotics rich and rare,
That to other eyes were lovelier,
But not to me so fair;
For those roses bright, O those roses bright!
I have twined them with my sister's locks,
That are hid in the dust from sight!

We had a well, a deep old well,
Where the spring was never dry,
And the cool drops down from the mossy stones
Were falling constantly:
And there never was water half so sweet
As that in my little cup,
Drawn up to the curb by the rude old sweep,
Which my father's hand set up;
And that deep old well, O that deep old well!
I remember yet the plashing sound
Of the bucket as it fell.

Our homestead had an ample hearth,
Where at night we loved to meet;

There my mother's voice was always kind,
    And her smile was always sweet;
And there I 've sat on my father's knee,
    And watched his thoughtful brow,
With my childish hand in his raven hair, —
    That hair is silver now!
But that broad hearth's light, O that broad hearth's light!
  And my father's look, and my mother's smile, —
They are in my heart to-night.

THE BOOK OF POEMS.

ON the pages whose rhymed music
  So oft has charmed thine ears,
I have gazed till my heart is filling
  With memories of vanished years;
And, leaving the lines of the poet,
  Has sadly turned to roam
Away to that beautiful valley
  In the sunset land of home!

O land of the greenest pastures,
  O land of the coolest streams,
Shall I only again be near you
  In the shadowy light of dreams?

Shall I only sit in visions
By the hearth and the lattice-pane,
And my friend of the past, my brother,
Shall we meet not there again?

As a sweet memorial ever
This book to my heart will be;
But I never can read its pages
So far from home and thee;
For the words grow dim before me,
Or tremble on my lips,
And the disc of life's orb of beauty
Is darkened with woe's eclipse.

So for ever closed and claspéd
Shall the volume lie unread,
As might in some ancient cloister
The gift of the saintly dead,
Till our hands shall open its pages
Once more beneath that dome
That hangs o'er the beautiful valley,
In the sunset land of home!

TO FRANK.

'T is three years and something over
  Since I looked upon you last,
But I only think about you
  As I saw you in the past.

And when memory recalls you,
  As she has done to day,
You 're just as young, and just as small,
  As when you went away.

I can see you hunt for flowers
  In the meadows green and sweet,
Or go wading through the hollows
  With your little, naked feet ; —

Or peeping through the bushes
  That hedged the garden round,
To see if any little birds
  Were in the nest you 'd found.

And I know how in the clover,
  Where the bees were used to come,
You held them down beneath your hat,
  To hear their pleasant hum.

And how in summer evenings,
  Through the door-yard wet with dew,
The watch-dog led you many a chase, —
  He 's growing older too!

I know when on the dear old porch
  We coaxed you first to walk,
And treasured every word you said
  When you began to talk.

We asked you what you meant to be,
  And laughed at your replies,
Because you said, when you grew up
  To manhood, you 'd be wise.

And may you pray the God of love,
  And I will pray him too,
To make you wise in every thing
  That makes man good and true!

PLEA FOR THE HOMELESS.

Columbia, fairest nation of the world,
  Sitting in queenly beauty in the west,
With all thy banners round about thee furled,
  Nursing the cherub Peace upon thy breast!
Never did daughter of a kingly line
Look on a lovelier heritage than thine!

Thou hast deep forests stretching far away,
  The giant growth of the long centuries,
From whose dim shadows to the light of day
  Come forth the mighty rivers toward the seas,
To walk like happy lovers, hand in hand,
Down through the green vales of our pleasant land.

Thou hast broad prairies, where the lonely flowers
  Blossom and perish with the changing year;

Where harvests wave not through the summer hours,
  Nor with the autumn ripen in the ear;
And beautiful lakes, that toss their milky spray
Where the strong ship hath never cleaved its way.

And yet, with all thy broad and fertile land,
  Where hands sow not, nor gather in the grain,
Thy children come and round about thee stand,
  Asking the blessing of a home in vain, —
Still lingering, but with feet that long to press
Through the green windings of the wilderness.

In populous cities do men live and die,
  That never breathe the pure and liberal air;
Down where the damp and desolate rice-swamps lie,
  Wearying the ear of Heaven with constant prayer,
Are souls that never yet have learned to raise
Under God's equal sky the psalm of praise.

Turn not, Columbia! from their pleading eyes;
  Give to thy sons that ask of thee a home;
So shall they gather round thee, not with sighs,
  But as young children to their mother come;
And brightly to the centuries shall go down
The glory that thou wearest like a crown.

MORNING.

Sadly, when the day was done,
To his setting waned the sun;
Heavily the shadows fell,
And the wind, with fitful swell,
Echoed through the forest dim
Like a friar's ghostly hymn.

Mournful on the wall, afar,
Walked the evening sentry-star;
Burning clear, and cold, and lone,
Midnight's constellations shone;
While the hours, with solemn tread,
Passed like watchers by the dead.

Now at last the Morning wakes,
And the spell of darkness breaks,

On the mountains, dewy sweet,
Standing with her rosy feet,
While her golden fingers fair
Part the soft flow of her hair.

With the dew from flower and leaf
Flies the heavy dew of grief;
From the darkness of my thought,
Night her solemn aspect caught;
And the morning's joys begin,
As a morning breaks within.

God's free sunshine on the hills,
Soft mists hanging o'er the rills,
Blushing flowers of loveliness
Trembling with the light wind's kiss, —
O, the soul forgets its care,
Looking on a world so fair!

Morning wooes me with her charms,
Like a lover's pleading arms;
Soft above me bend her skies,
As a lover's tender eyes;
And my heavy heart of pain,
Trembling, thrills with hope again.

DAWN.

THE sunken moon was down an hour agone ; —
  And now the little silver cloud, that leant
  So lovingly above her as she went,
Is changing with the touches of the dawn :
For from the claspèd arms of the sweet night,
  Lo ! the young Dawn has gently stolen away,
  And stars, that late burned with an intense ray,
Fade to a wannish, melancholy light.
A moment, smiling on the hills she stands,
  Parting the curtains of the East away ;
Then lightly, with her white caressing hands,
  Touches the trembling eyelids of the Day ;
And, leaning o'er his couch of rosy beams,
Wooes him with kisses softly from his dreams.

PARODIES.

MARTHA HOPKINS.

A BALLAD OF INDIANA.

From the kitchen, Martha Hopkins, as she stands there making pies,
Southward looks, along the turnpike, with her hand above her eyes;
Where, along the distant hill-side, her yearling heifer feeds,
And a little grass is growing in a mighty sight of weeds.

All the air is full of noises, for there is n't any school,
And boys, with turned-up pantaloons, are wading in the pool;
Blithely frisk unnumbered chickens, cackling, for they cannot laugh;
Where the airy summits brighten, nimbly leaps the little calf.

Gentle eyes of Martha Hopkins! tell me wherefore do ye gaze
On the ground that 's being furrowed for the planting of the maize?
Tell me wherefore down the valley ye have traced the turnpike's way,
Far beyond the cattle-pasture, and the brickyard, with its clay?

Ah! the dog-wood tree may blossom, and the door-yard grass may shine,
With the tears of amber dropping from the washing on the line,
And the morning's breath of balsam lightly brush her freckled cheek, —
Little recketh Martha Hopkins of the tales of spring they speak.

When the summer's burning solstice on the scanty harvest glowed,
She had watched a man on horseback riding down the turnpike-road;
Many times she saw him turning, looking backward quite forlorn,
Till amid her tears she lost him, in the shadow of the barn.

Ere the supper-time was over, he had passed the kiln
of brick,
Crossed the rushing Yellow River, and had forded quite
a creek,
And his flatboat load was taken, at the time for pork
and beans,
With the traders of the Wabash, to the wharf at New
Orleans.

Therefore watches Martha Hopkins, holding in her
hand the pans,
When the sound of distant footsteps seems exactly like
a man's;
Not a wind the stove-pipe rattles, nor a door behind her
jars,
But she seems to hear the rattle of his letting down the
bars.

Often sees she men on horseback, coming down the
turnpike rough,
But they come not as John Jackson, she can see it well
enough;
Well she knows the sober trotting of the sorrel horse
he keeps,
As he jogs along at leisure, with his head down like a
sheep's.

She would know him 'mid a thousand, by his home-made
coat and vest;
By his socks, which were blue woollen, such as farmers
wear out west;
By the color of his trousers, and his saddle, which was
spread
By a blanket which was taken for that purpose from
the bed.

None like he the yoke of hickory on the unbroken ox
can throw,
None amid his father's cornfields use like him the
spade and hoe;
And at all the apple-cuttings, few indeed the men are
seen,
That can dance with him the Polka, touch with him the
violin.

He has said to Martha Hopkins, and she thinks she
hears him now,
For she knows as well as can be, that he meant to keep
his vow,
When the buckeye tree has blossomed, and your uncle
plants his corn,
Shall the bells of Indiana usher in the wedding morn.

He has pictured his relations, each in Sunday hat and
gown,
And he thinks he 'll get a carriage, and they 'll spend
a day in town;
That their love will newly kindle, and what comfort it
will give,
To sit down to the first breakfast, in the cabin where
they 'll live.

Tender eyes of Martha Hopkins! what has got you in
such scrape?
'T is a tear that falls to glitter on the ruffle of her
cape.
Ah! the eye of love may brighten, to be certain what
it sees,
One man looks much like another, when half hidden
by the trees.

But her eager eyes rekindle, she forgets the pies and
bread,
As she sees a man on horseback, round the corner of
the shed.
Now tie on another apron, get the comb and smooth
your hair,
'T is the sorrel horse that gallops, 't is John Jackson's
self that 's there!

WORSER MOMENTS.

THAT fellow's voice ! how often steals
  Its cadence o'er my lonely days !
Like something sent on wagon-wheels,
  Or packed in an unconscious chaise.
I might forget the words he said
  When all the children fret and cry,
But when I get them off to bed,
  His gentle tone comes stealing by,
And years of matrimony flee,
And leave me sitting on his knee.

The times he came to court a spell,
  The tender things he said to me,
Make me remember mighty well
  My hopes that he 'd propose to me.

My face is uglier, and perhaps
  Time and the comb have thinned my hair,
And plain and common are the caps
  And dresses that I have to wear;
But memory is ever yet
With all that fellow's flatteries writ.

I have been out at milking-time
  Beneath a dull and rainy sky,
When in the barn 't was time to feed,
  And calves were bawling lustily, —
When scattered hay, and sheaves of oats,
  And yellow corn-ears, sound and hard,
And all that makes the cattle pass
  With wilder fleetness through the yard, —
When all was hateful, then have I,
  With friends who had to help me milk,
Talked of his wife most spitefully,
  And how he kept her dressed in silk;
And when the cattle, running there,
  Threw over me a shower of mud,
That fellow's voice came on the air,
  Like the light chewing of the cud,
And resting near some speckled cow,
  The spirit of a woman's spite,

I 've poured a low and fervent vow
  To make him, if I had the might,
Live all his lifetime just as hard,
And milk his cows in such a yard.

I have been out to pick up wood,
  When night was stealing from the dawn,
Before the fire was burning good,
  Or I had put the kettle on
The little stove, — when babes were waking
  With a low murmur in the beds,
And melody by fits was breaking
  Above their little yellow heads, —
And this when I was up perhaps
From a few short and troubled naps, —
  And when the sun sprang scorchingly
And freely up, and made us stifle,
  And fell upon each hill and tree
The bullets from his subtle rifle, —
  I say a voice has thrilled me then,
Hard by that solemn pile of wood,
  Or creeping from the silent glen,
Like something on the unfledged brood,
  Hath stricken me, and I have pressed
Close in my arms my load of chips,

And pouring forth the hatefulest
Of words that ever passed my lips,
Have felt my woman's spirit rush
On me, as on that milking night,
And, yielding to the blessed gush
Of my ungovernable spite,
Have risen up, the wed, the old,
Scolding as hard as I could scold.

THE ANNOYER.

"Common as light is love,
And its familiar voice wearies not ever." — Shelley.

Love knoweth everybody's house,
  And every human haunt,
And comes unbidden everywhere,
  Like people we don't want.
The turnpike-roads and little creeks
  Are written with love's words,
And you hear his voice like a thousand bricks
  In the lowing of the herds.

He peeps into the teamster's heart,
  From his Buena Vista's rim,
And the cracking whips of many men
  Can never frighten him.

He 'll come to his cart in the weary night,
  When he 's dreaming of his craft ;
And he 'll float to his eye in the morning light,
  Like a man on a river raft.

He hears the sound of the cooper's adze,
  And makes him too his dupe,
For he sighs in his ear from the shaving pile,
  As he hammers on the hoop.
The little girl, the beardless boy,
  The men that walk or stand,
He will get them all in his mighty arms,
  Like the grasp of your very hand.

The shoemaker bangs above his bench,
  And ponders his shining awl,
For love is under the lapstone hid,
  And a spell is on the wall.
It heaves the sole where he drives the pegs,
  And speaks in every blow,
Till the last is dropped from his crafty hand
  And his foot hangs bare below.

He blurs the prints which the shopmen sell,
  And intrudes on the hatter's trade,

10

And profanes the hostler's stable-yard
  In the shape of the chamber-maid.
In the darkest night and the bright daylight,
  Knowing that he can win,
In every home of good-looking folks
  Will human love come in.

SAMUEL BROWN.

It was many and many a year ago,
  In a dwelling down in town,
That a fellow there lived whom you may know,
  By the name of Samuel Brown;
And this fellow he lived with no other thought
  Than to our house to come down.

I was a child, and he was a child,
  In that dwelling down in town,
But we loved with a love that was more than love,
  I and my Samuel Brown, —
With a love that the ladies coveted,
  Me and Samuel Brown.

And this was the reason that, long ago,
  To that dwelling down in town,
A girl came out of her carriage, courting
  My beautiful Samuel Brown;
So that her high-bred kinsman came
  And bore away Samuel Brown,
And shut him up in a dwelling-house,
  In a street quite up in town.

The ladies not half so happy up there,
  Went envying me and Brown;
Yes! that was the reason, (as all men know,
  In this dwelling down in town,)
That the girl came out of the carriage by night,
  Coquetting and getting my Samuel Brown.

But our love is more artful by far than the love
  Of those who are older than we, —
  Of many far wiser than we, —
And neither the girls that are living above,
  Nor the girls that are down in town,
Can ever dissever my soul from the soul
  Of the beautiful Samuel Brown.

For the morn never shines without bringing me lines
  From my beautiful Samuel Brown;

And the night 's never dark, but I sit in the park
  With my beautiful Samuel Brown.
And often by day, I walk down in Broadway,
With my darling, my darling, my life and my stay,
  To our dwelling down in town,
To our house in the street down town.

GRANNY'S HOUSE.

Comrades, leave me here a little, while as yet 't is
early morn,
Leave me here, and when you want me, sound upon
the dinner-horn.
'T is the place, and all about it, as of old, the rat and
mouse
Very loudly squeak and nibble, running over Granny's
house; —
Granny's house, with all its cupboards, and its rooms
as neat as wax,
And its chairs of wood unpainted, where the old cats
rubbed their backs.
Many a night from yonder garret window, ere I went
to rest,
Did I see the cows and horses come in slowly from the
west;

Many a night I saw the chickens, flying upward through the trees,
Roosting on the sleety branches, when I thought their feet would freeze;
Here about the garden wandered, nourishing a youth sublime
With the beans, and sweet potatoes, and the melons which were prime;
When the pumpkin-vines behind me with their precious fruit reposed,
When I clung about the pear-tree, for the promise that it closed,
When I dipt into the dinner far as human eye could see,
Saw the vision of the pie, and all the dessert that would be.

In the spring a fuller crimson comes upon the robin's breast;
In the spring the noisy pullet gets herself another nest;
In the spring a livelier spirit makes the ladies' tongues more glib;
In the spring a young boy's fancy lightly hatches up a fib.

Then her cheek was plump and fatter than should be for one so old,
And she eyed my every motion, with a mute intent to scold.

And I said, My worthy Granny, now I speak the truth
to thee, —
Better believe it, — I have eaten all the apples from one
tree.
On her kindling cheek and forehead came a color and
a light,
As I have seen the rosy red flashing in the northern
night;
And she turned, — her fist was shaken at the coolness
of the lie;
She was mad, and I could see it, by the snapping of
her eye,
Saying I have hid my feelings, fearing they should do
thee wrong, —
Saying, "I shall whip you, Sammy, whipping, I shall
go it strong!"
She took me up and turned me pretty roughly, when
she 'd done,
And every time she shook me, I tried to jerk and
run;
She took off my little coat, and struck again with all
her might,
And before another minute I was free and out of
sight.
Many a morning, just to tease her, did I tell her stories
yet,

Though her whisper made me tingle, when she told me
what I 'd get ;
Many an evening did I see her where the willow sprouts
grew thick,
And I rushed away from Granny at the touching of her
stick.
O my Granny, old and ugly, O my Granny's hatefnl
deeds,
O the empty, empty garret, O the garden gone to
weeds,
Crosser than all fancy fathoms, crosser than all songs
have sung,
I was puppet to your threat, and servile to your shrew-
ish tongue,
Is it well to wish thee happy, having seen thy whip
decline
On a boy with lower shoulders, and a narrower back,
than mine ?
Hark, my merry comrades call me, sounding on the
dinner-horn, —
They to whom my Granny's whippings were a target
for their scorn ;
Shall it not be scorn to me to harp on such a mouldered
string ?
I am shamed through all my nature to have loved the
mean old thing ;

Weakness to be wroth with weakness! woman's pleasure, woman's spite,
Nature made them quicker motions, a considerable sight.
Woman is the lesser man, and all thy whippings matched with mine
Are as moonlight unto sunlight, and as water unto wine.
Here at least when I was little, something, O, for some retreat
Deep in yonder crowded city where my life began to beat,
Where one winter fell my father, slipping off a keg of lard,
I was left a trampled orphan, and my case was pretty hard.
Or to burst all links of habit, and to wander far and fleet,
On from farm-house unto farm-house till I found my Uncle Pete,
Larger sheds and barns, and newer, and a better neighborhood,
Greater breadth of field and woodland, and an orchard just as good.
Never comes my Granny, never cuts her willow switches there;

Boys are safe at Uncle Peter's, I 'll bet you what you
dare.
Hangs the heavy fruited pear-tree : you may eat just
what you like.
'T is a sort of little Eden, about two miles off the
pike.
There, methinks, would be enjoyment, more than being
quite so near
To the place where even in manhood I almost shake
with fear.
There the passions, cramped no longer, shall have
scope and breathing space.
I will 'scape that savage woman, she shall never rear
my race ;
Iron-jointed, supple-sinewed, they shall dive and they
shall run ;
She has caught me like a wild goat, but she shall not
catch my son.
He shall whistle to the dog, and get the books from off
the shelf,
Not, with blinded eyesight, cutting ugly whips to whip
himself.
Fool again, the dream of fancy ! no, I don't believe
it 's bliss,
But I 'm certain Uncle Peter's is a better place than
this.

Let them herd with narrow foreheads, vacant of all glorious gains,
Like the horses in the stables, like the sheep that crop the lanes;
Let them mate with dirty cousins, — what to me were style or rank,
I the heir of twenty acres, and some money in the bank?
Not in vain the distance beckons, forward let us urge our load,
Let our cart-wheels spin till sun-down, ringing down the grooves of road;
Through the white dust of the turnpike she can't see to give us chase:
Better seven years at uncle's, than fourteen at Granny's place.
O, I see the blessed promise of my spirit hath not set!
If we once get in the wagon, we will circumvent her yet.
Howsoever these things, be a long farewell to Granny's farm:
Not for me she 'll cut the willows, not at me she 'll shake her arm.
Comes a vapor from the margin, blackening over heath and holt,

Cramming all the blast before it,—guess it holds a thunderbolt:
Wish 't would fall on Granny's house, with rain, or hail, or fire, or snow,
Let me get my horses started Uncle Peteward, and I'll go.

"THE DAY IS DONE."

THE day is done, and darkness
  From the wing of night is loosed,
As a feather is wafted downward
  From a chicken going to roost.

I see the lights of the baker
  Gleam through the rain and mist,
And a feeling of sadness comes o'er me,
  That I cannot well resist.

A feeling of sadness and *longing*,
  That is not like being sick,
And resembles sorrow only
  As a brick-bat resembles a brick.

Come, get for me some supper, —
  A good and regular meal,
That shall soothe this restless feeling,
  And banish the pain I feel.

Not from the pastry baker's,
  Not from the shops for cake,
I would n't give a farthing
  For all that they can make.

For, like the soup at dinner,
  Such things would but suggest
Some dishes more substantial,
  And to-night I want the best.

Go to some honest butcher,
  Whose beef is fresh and nice
As any they have in the city,
  And get a liberal slice.

Such things through days of labor,
  And nights devoid of ease,
For sad and desperate feelings
  Are wonderful remedies.

They have an astonishing power
  To aid and reinforce,
And come like the "Finally, brethren,"
  That follows a long discourse.

Then get me a tender sirloin
  From off the bench or hook,
And lend to its sterling goodness
  The science of the cook.

And the night shall be filled with comfort,
  And the cares with which it begun
Shall fold up their blankets like Indians,
  And silently cut and run.

JOHN THOMPSON'S DAUGHTER.

A FELLOW near Kentucky's clime
Cries, " Boatman, do not tarry,
And I 'll give thee a silver dime
To row us o'er the ferry."

" Now, who would cross the Ohio,
This dark and stormy water ? "
" O, I am this young lady's beau,
And she John Thompson's daughter.

" We 've fled before her father's spite
With great precipitation,
And should he find us here to-night,
I 'd lose my reputation.

"They 've missed the girl and purse beside,
His horsemen hard have pressed me,
And who will cheer my bonny bride,
If yet they shall arrest me?"

Out spoke the boatman then in time,
"You shall not fail, don't fear it;
I 'll go, not for your silver dime,
But for your manly spirit.

"And by my word, the bonny bird
In danger shall not tarry;
For though a storm is coming on,
I 'll row you o'er the ferry."

By this the wind more fiercely rose,
The boat was at the landing,
And with the drenching rain their clothes
Grew wet where they were standing.

But still, as wilder rose the wind,
And as the night grew drearer,
Just back a piece came the police,
Their tramping sounded nearer.

" O, haste thee, haste ! " the lady cries,
" It 's any thing but funny ;
I 'll leave the light of loving eyes,
But not my father's money ! "

And still they hurried in the face
Of wind and rain unsparing ;
John Thompson reached the landing-place,
His wrath was turned to swearing.

For by the lightning's angry flash,
His child he did discover ;
One lovely hand held all his cash,
And one was round her lover !

" Come back, come back," he cried in woe,
Across the stormy water ;
" But leave the purse, and you may go,
My daughter, O my daughter ! "

'T was vain ; they reached the other shore,
(Such dooms the Fates assign us,)
The gold he piled went with his child,
And he was left there, *minus*.

GIRLS WERE MADE TO MOURN.

When chill November's surly blast
Made everybody shiver,
One evening as I wandered forth,
Along the Wabash River,
I spied a woman past her prime,
Yet with a youthful air,
Her face was covered o'er with curls
Of *well-selected* hair !

Young woman, whither wanderest thou ?
Began the prim old maid ;
Are visions of a home to be,
In all thy dreams displayed ?
Or haply wanting but a mate,
Too soon thou hast began
To wander forth with me to mourn
The indifference of man !

The sun that overhangs yon fields,
  Outspreading far and wide,
Where thousands by their own hearth sit,
  Or in their carriage ride, —
I 've seen yon weary winter sun
  Just forty times return;
And every time has added proofs,
  That girls were made to mourn!

O girls! when in your early years,
  How prodigal of time!
Misspending all your precious hours,
  Your glorious youthful prime!
Thinking to wed just when you please,
  From beau to beau you turn,
Which tenfold force gives nature's law,
  That girls were made to mourn!

Look not on them in youthful prime,
  Ere life's best years are spent!
Man will be gallant to them then,
  And give encouragement!
But see them when they cease to speak
  Of each birthday's return;
Then want and single-blessedness
  Show girls were made to mourn!

A few seem favorites of fate,
  By husband's hands caressed,
But think not all the married folks
  Are likewise truly blest.
For, oh ! what crowds, whose lords are out,
  That stay to patch and darn,
Through weary life this lesson learn,
  That girls were made to mourn !

Many and sharp and numerous ills,
  Inwoven with our frame !
More pointed still we make ourselves,
  Regret, remorse, and shame !
And man, whose heaven-erected face
  The smiles of love adorn,—
Man's cold indifference to us
  Makes countless thousands mourn !

If I 'm designed to live alone,—
  By nature's law designed,—
Why was this constant wish to wed
  E'er planted in my mind ?
If not, why am I subject to
  Man's cruelty or scorn ?
Or why has he the will and power
  To make me for him mourn ?

See yonder young, accomplished girl,
  Whose words are smooth as oil,
Who 'd marry almost any one
  To keep her hands from toil;
But see, the lordly gentleman
  Her favors don't return,
Unmindful though a weeping ma
  And bankrupt father mourn!

Yet let not this, my hopeful girl,
  Disturb thy youthful breast;
This awful view of woman's fate
  Is surely not the best!
The poor, despisèd, plain old maid
  Had never sure been born,
Had there not been some recompense
  To comfort those who mourn!

O death! the poor girl's dearest friend,
  The kindest and the best!
Welcome the hour my weary limbs
  Are laid with thee to rest!
The young, the married, fear thy blow
  From hope or husbands torn;
But oh! a blest relief to those
  In single life who mourn!

TO INEZ.

NAY, smile not at my garments now;
Alas! *I* cannot smile again:
Yet Heaven avert that ever thou
Shouldst dress, and haply dress so plain.

And dost thou ask, Why should I be
The jest of every foe and friend?
And wilt thou vainly seek to see
A garb, even thou must fail to mend?

It is not love, it is not hate,
Nor low Ambition's honors lost,
That bids me loathe my present state,
And fly from all I loved the most:

It is the contrast which will spring
  From all I meet, or hear, or see :
To me no garments tailors bring,—
  Their shops have scarce a charm for me.

It is a something all who rub
  Would know the owner long had wore ;
That may not look beyond the tub,
  And cannot hope for help before.

What fellow from himself can flee ?
  To zones, though more and more remote,
Still, still pursues, where'er I be,
  The blight of life,—the ragged Coat.

Yet others wrapt in broadcloth seem,
  And taste of all that I forsake !
O, may they still of transport dream,
  And ne'er, at least like me, awake !

Through many a clime 't is mine to go,
  With many a retrospection curst ;
And all my solace is to know,
  Whate'er I wear, I 've worn the worst.

What is that worst ? Nay, do not ask, —
  In pity from the search forbear :
Smile on, — nor venture to unclasp
  My Vest, and view the Shirt that 's there.

TO MARY.

WELL! thou art happy, and I say
  That I should thus be happy too;
For still I hate to go away
  As badly as I used to do.

Thy husband 's blest,— and 't will impart
  Some pangs to view his happier lot;
But let them pass,— O, how my heart
  Would hate him, if he clothed thee not!

When late I saw thy favorite child,
  I thought, like Dutchmen, "I 'd go dead,"
But when I saw its breakfast piled,
  I thought how much 't would take for bread.

I saw it, and repressed my groans
  Its father in its face to see,
Because I knew my scanty funds
  Were scarce enough for you and me.

Mary, adieu! I must away;
  While thou art blest, to grieve were sin,
But near thee I can never stay,
  Because I 'd get in love again.

I deemed that time, I deemed that pride,
  My boyish feeling had subdued,
Nor knew, till seated by thy side,
  I 'd try to get you, if I could.

Yet was I calm: I recollect,
  My hand had once sought yours again,
But now your husband might object,
  And so I kept it on my cane.

I saw thee gaze upon my face,
  Yet meet with neither woe nor scoff;
One only feeling couldst thou trace,
  A disposition to be off.

Away! away, my early dream,
  Remembrance never must awake;
O, where is Mississippi's stream?
  My foolish heart, be still, or break!

THE CHANGE.

In sunset's light o'er Boston thrown,
  A young man proudly stood
Beside a girl, the only one
  He thought was fair or good;
The one on whom his heart was set,
The one he tried so long to get.

He heard his wife's first loving sound,
  A low, mysterious tone,
A music sought, but never found,
  By beaux and gallants gone;
He listened and his heart beat high,—
That was the song of victory!

The rapture of the conqueror's mood
  Rushed burning through his frame,
And all the folks that round him stood
  Its torrents could not tame,
Though stillness lay with eve's last smile
Round Boston Common all the while.

Years came with care ; across his life
  There swept a sudden change,
E'en with the one he called his wife,
  A shadow dark and strange,
Breathed from the thought so swift to fall
O'er triumph's hour, — and is this all ?

No, more than this! what seemed it *now*
  Right by that one to stand ?
A thousand girls of fairer brow
  Walked his own mountain land ;
Whence, far o'er matrimony's track,
Their wild, sweet voices called him back.

They called him back to many a glade
  Where once he joyed to rove,
Where often in the beechen shade
  He sat and talked of love ;

They called him with their mocking sport
Back to the times he used to court.

But, darkly mingling with the thought
  Of each remembered scene,
Rose up a fearful vision, fraught
  With all that lay between, —
His wrinkled face, his altered lot,
His children's wants, the wife he'd got!

Where was the value of that bride
  He likened once to pearls?
His weary heart within him died
  With yearning for the girls, —
All vainly struggling to repress
That gush of painful tenderness.

He wept; the wife that made his bread
  Beheld the sad reverse,
Even on the spot where he had said
  "For better or for worse."
O happiness! how far we flee
Thine own sweet path in search of thee!

"HE NEVER WROTE AGAIN."

His hope of publishing went down,
  The sweeping press rolled on;
But what was any other crown
  To him who had n't one?
He lived, — for long may man bewail
  When thus he writes in vain:
Why comes not death to those who fail: —
  He never wrote again!

Books were put out, and "had a run,"
  Like coinage from the mint;
But which could fill the place of one,
  That one they would n't print?

Before him passed, in calf and sheep,
  The thoughts of many a brain :
His lay with the rejected heap : —
  He never wrote again !

He sat where men who wrote went round,
  And heard the rhymes they built ;
He saw their works most richly bound,
  With portraits and in gilt.
Dreams of a volume all forgot
  Were blent with every strain :
A thought of one they issued not : —
  He never wrote again !

Minds in that time closed o'er the trace
  Of books once fondly read,
And others came to fill their place,
  And were perused instead.
Tales which young girls had bathed in tears
  Back on the shelves were lain :
Fresh ones came out for other years : —
  He never wrote again !

THE SOIREE.

This is the Soiree : from grate to entrance,
  Like milliners' figures, stand the lovely girls ;
But from their silent lips no merry sentence
  Disturbs the smoothness of their shining curls.

Ah ! what will rise, how will they rally,
  When shall arrive the " gentlemen of ease " !
What brilliant repartee, what witty sally,
  Will mingle with their pleasant symphonies !

I hear even now the infinite sweet chorus,
  The laugh of ecstasy, the merry tone,
That through the evenings that have gone before us
  In long reverberations reach our own.

From round-faced Germans come the guttural voices,
Through curling *moustache* steals the Italian clang,
And, loud amidst their universal noises,
From distant corners sounds the Yankee twang.

I hear the editor, who from his office
Sends out his paper, filled with praise and puff,
And holy priests, who, when they warn the scoffers,
Beat the fine pulpit, lined with velvet stuff.

The tumult of each *saqued*, and charming maiden,
The idle talk that sense and reason drowns,
The ancient dames with jewelry o'erladen,
And trains depending from the brocade gowns, —

The pleasant tone, whose sweetness makes us wonder,
The laugh of gentlemen, and ladies too,
And ever and anon, in tones of thunder,
The diapason of some lady *blue*, —

Is it, O man, with such discordant noises,
With pastimes so ridiculous as these,
Thou drownest Nature's sweet and kindly voices,
And jarrest the celestial harmonies?

Were half the wealth that fills the world with ladies,
  Were half the time bestowed on caps and lace,
Given to the home, the husbands, and the babies,
  There were no time to visit such a place.

THE CITY LIFE.

How shall I know thee in that sphere that keeps
  The country youth that to the city goes,
When all of thee, that change can wither, sleeps
  And perishes among your cast-off clothes?

For I shall feel the sting of ceaseless pain,
  If there I meet thy one-horse carriage not;
Nor see the hat I love, nor ride again,
  When thou art driving on a gentle trot.

Wilt thou not for me in the city seek,
  And turn to note each passing shawl and gown?
You used to come and see me once a week,—
  Shall I be banished from your thought in town?

In that great street I don't know how to find,
  In the resplendence of that glorious sphere,
And larger movements of the unfettered mind,
  Wilt thou forget the love that joined us here?

The love that lived through all the simple past,
  And meekly with my country training bore,
And deeper grew, and tenderer to the last,
  Shall it expire in town, and be no more?

A happier lot than mine, and greater praise,
  Await thee there; for thou, with skill and tact,
Hast learnt the wisdom of the world's just ways,
  And dressest well, and knowest how to act.

For me, the country place in which I dwell
  Has made me one of a proscribed band;
And work hath left its scar — that fire of hell
  Has left its frightful scar upon my hand.

Yet though thou wear'st the glory of the town,
  Wilt thou not keep the same belovèd name,
The same black-satin vest, and morning-gown,
  Lovelier in New York city, yet the same?

Shalt thou not teach me, in that grander home
  The wisdom that I learned so ill in this, —
The wisdom which is fine, — till I become
  Thy fit companion in that place of bliss?

THE MARRIAGE OF SIR JOHN SMITH.

Not a sigh was heard, nor a funeral tone,
As the man to his bridal we hurried ;
Not a woman discharged her farewell groan,
On the spot where the fellow was married.

We married him just about eight at night,
Our faces paler turning,
By the struggling moonbeam's misty light,
And the gas-lamp's steady burning.

No useless watch-chain covered his vest,
Nor over-dressed we found him ;
But he looked like a gentleman wearing his best,
With a few of his friends around him.

Few and short were the things we said,
 And we spoke not a word of sorrow,
But we silently gazed on the man that was wed,
 And we bitterly thought of the morrow.

We thought, as we silently stood about,
 With spite and anger dying,
How the merest stranger had cut us out,
 With only half our trying.

Lightly we 'll talk of the fellow that 's gone,
 And oft for the past upbraid him ;
But little he 'll reck if we let him live on,
 In the house where his wife conveyed him.

But our heavy task at length was done,
 When the clock struck the hour for retiring ;
And we heard the spiteful squib and pun
 The girls were sullenly firing.

Slowly and sadly we turned to go, —
 We had struggled, and we were human ;
We shed not a tear, and we spoke not our woe,
 But we left him alone with his woman.

BALLAD OF THE CANAL.

We were crowded in the cabin,
  Not a soul had room to sleep ;
It was midnight on the waters,
  And the banks were very steep.

'T is a fearful thing when sleeping
  To be startled by the shock,
And to hear the rattling trumpet
  Thunder, " Coming to a lock ! "

So we shuddered there in silence,
  For the stoutest berth was shook,
While the wooden gates were opened
  And the mate talked with the cook.

As thus we lay in darkness,
Each one wishing we were there,
" We are through ! " the captain shouted,
And he sat down on a chair.

And his little daughter whispered,
Thinking that he ought to know,
" Is n't travelling by canal-boats
Just as safe as it is slow ? "

Then he kissed the little maiden,
And with better cheer we spoke,
And we trotted into Pittsburg
When the morn looked through the smoke.

I REMEMBER, I REMEMBER.

I REMEMBER, I remember,
The house where I was wed,
And the little room from which, that night,
My smiling bride was led;
She did n't come a wink too soon,
Nor make too long a stay;
But now I often wish her folks
Had kept the girl away!

I remember, I remember,
Her dresses, red and white,
Her bonnets and her caps and cloaks, —
They cost an awful sight!

The " corner lot " on which I built,
  And where my brother met
At first my wife, one washing-day, —
  That man is single yet !

I remember, I remember,
  Where I was used to court,
And thought that all of married life
  Was just such pleasant sport :
My spirit flew in feathers then,
  No care was on my brow ;
I scarce could wait to shut the gate, —
  I 'm not so anxious now !

I remember, I remember,
  My dear one's smile and sigh ;
I used to think her tender heart
  Was close against the sky ;
It was a childish ignorance,
  But now it soothes me not
To know I 'm farther off from heaven
  Than when she was n't got !

JACOB.

He dwelt among "apartments let,"
About five stories high;
A man I thought that none would get,
And very few would try.

A boulder, by a larger stone
Half hidden in the mud,
Fair as a man when only one
Is in the neighborhood.

He lived unknown, and few could tell
When Jacob was not free;
But he has got a wife, — and O!
The difference to me!

THE WIFE.

Her washing ended with the day,
Yet lived she at its close,
And passed the long, long night away,
In darning ragged hose.

But when the sun in all his state
Illumed the eastern skies,
She passed about the kitchen grate,
And went to making pies.

A PSALM OF LIFE.

WHAT THE HEART OF THE YOUNG WOMAN SAID TO THE OLD MAID.

TELL me not, in idle jingle,
Marriage is an empty dream,
For the girl is dead that 's single,
And things are not what they seem.

Married life is real, earnest;
Single blessedness a fib;
Taken from man, to man returnest,
Has been spoken of the rib.

Not enjoyment, and not sorrow,
Is our destined end or way;
But to act, that each to-morrow
Nearer brings the wedding-day.

13

Life is long, and youth is fleeting,
  And our hearts, if there we search,
Still like steady drums are beating
  Anxious marches to the church.

In the world's broad field of battle,
  In the bivouac of life,
Be not like dumb, driven cattle !
  Be a woman, be a wife !

Trust no Future, howe'er pleasant !
  Let the dead Past bury its dead !
Act, — act in the living Present :
  Heart within, and MAN ahead !

Lives of married folks remind us
  We can live our lives as well,
And, departing, leave behind us
  Such examples as will tell ; —

Such examples, that another,
  Sailing far from Hymen's port,
A forlorn, unmarried brother,
  Seeing, shall take heart, and court.

Let us then be up and doing,
  With the heart and head begin;
Still achieving, still pursuing,
  Learn to labor, and to win!

"THERE 'S A BOWER OF BEAN-VINES."

THERE 's a bower of bean-vines in Benjamin's yard,
And the cabbages grow round it, planted for greens;
In the time of my childhood 't was terribly hard
To bend down the bean-poles, and pick off the beans.

That bower and its products I never forget,
But oft, when my landlady presses me hard,
I think, are the cabbages growing there yet,
Are the bean-vines still bearing in Benjamin's yard?

No, the bean-vines soon withered that once used to wave,
But some beans had been gathered, the last that hung on,
And a soup was distilled in a kettle, that gave
All the fragrance of summer when summer was gone.

Thus memory draws from delight, ere it dies,
  An essence that breathes of it awfully hard;
And thus good to my taste as 't was then to my eyes,
  Is that bower of bean-vines in Benjamin's yard.

"WHEN LOVELY WOMAN."

When lovely woman wants a favor,
  And finds, too late, that man wont bend,
What earthly circumstance can save her
  From disappointment in the end?

The only way to bring him over,
  The last experiment to try,
Whether a husband or a lover,
  If he have feeling, is, to cry!

SHAKESPEARIAN READINGS.

OH, but to fade, and live we know not where,
To be a cold obstruction and to groan!
This sensible, warm woman, to become
A prudish clod; and the delighted spirit
To live and die alone, or to reside
With married sisters, and to have the care
Of half a dozen children, not your own;
And driven, for no one wants you,
Round about the pendant world; or worse than worst
Of those that disappointment and pure spite
Have driven to madness: 'T is too horrible!
The weariest and most troubled married life
That age, ache, penury, or jealousy
Can lay on nature, is a paradise
To being an old maid.

That very time I saw, (but thou couldst not,)
Walking between the garden and the barn,
Reuben, all armed ; a certain aim he took
At a young chicken, standing by a post,
And loosed his bullet smartly from his gun,
As he would kill a hundred thousand hens.
But I might see young Reuben's fiery shot
Lodged in the chaste board of the garden fence,
And the domesticated fowl passed on,
In henly meditation, bullet free.

My father had a daughter got a man,
As it might be, perhaps, were I good-looking,
I should, your lordship.
And what 's her residence ?
A hut, my lord, she never owned a house,
But let her husband, like a graceless scamp,
Spend all her little means,—she thought she ought,—
And in a wretched chamber, on an alley,
She worked like masons on a monument,
Earning their bread. Was not this love indeed ?

HENRY W. LONGFELLOW'S WRITINGS.

THE GOLDEN LEGEND. A Poem. Just Published. Price $1.00.

POETICAL WORKS. This edition contains the six Volumes mentioned below. In two volumes. 16mo. Boards. $2.00.

In separate Volumes, each 75 cents.

VOICES OF THE NIGHT.

BALLADS AND OTHER POEMS.

SPANISH STUDENT; A PLAY IN THREE ACTS.

BELFRY OF BRUGES, AND OTHER POEMS.

EVANGELINE; A TALE OF ACADIE.

THE SEASIDE AND THE FIRESIDE.

THE WAIF. A Collection of Poems. Edited by Longfellow.

THE ESTRAY. A Collection of Poems. Edited by Longfellow.

MR. LONGFELLOW'S PROSE WORKS.

HYPERION. A ROMANCE. Price $1.00.

OUTRE-MER. A PILGRIMAGE. Price $1.00.

KAVANAGH. A TALE. Price 75 cents.

Illustrated editions of THE POEMS and HYPERION.

NATHANIEL HAWTHORNE'S WRITINGS.

TWICE-TOLD TALES. Two Volumes. Price $1.50.

THE SCARLET LETTER. Price 75 cents.

THE HOUSE OF THE SEVEN GABLES. Price $1.00.

THE SNOW IMAGE, AND OTHER TWICE-TOLD TALES. Price 75 cents.

THE BLITHEDALE ROMANCE. Price 75 cents.

TRUE STORIES FROM HISTORY AND BIOGRAPHY. With four fine Engravings. Price 75 cents.

A WONDER-BOOK FOR GIRLS AND BOYS. With seven fine Engravings. Price 75 cents.

TANGLEWOOD TALES. Another 'Wonder-Book.' With Engravings. Price 88 cents.

JOHN G. WHITTIER'S WRITINGS.

OLD PORTRAITS AND MODERN SKETCHES. 75 cents.

MARGARET SMITH'S JOURNAL. Price 75 cents.

SONGS OF LABOR, AND OTHER POEMS. Boards. 50 cts.

THE CHAPEL OF THE HERMITS. Cloth. 50 cents.

JAMES RUSSELL LOWELL'S WRITINGS.

COMPLETE POETICAL WORKS. Revised, with Additions. In two volumes, 16mo. Cloth Price $1.50.

SIR LAUNFAL. New Edition. Price 25 cents.

THE BIGLOW PAPERS. A New Edition. Price 63 cents.

EDWIN P. WHIPPLE'S WRITINGS.

ESSAYS AND REVIEWS. 2 Vols. Price $2.00.

LECTURES ON SUBJECTS CONNECTED WITH LITERATURE AND LIFE. Price 63 cents.

WASHINGTON AND THE REVOLUTION. Price 20 cts.

OLIVER WENDELL HOLMES'S WRITINGS.

POETICAL WORKS. With fine Portrait. Boards. $1.00.

ASTRÆA. Fancy paper. Price 25 cents.

GRACE GREENWOOD'S WRITINGS.

GREENWOOD LEAVES. 1st & 2d Series. $1.25 each.

POETICAL WORKS. With fine Portrait. Price 75 cents.

HISTORY OF MY PETS. With six fine Engravings. Scarlet cloth. Price 50 cents.

RECOLLECTIONS OF MY CHILDHOOD. With six fine Engravings. Scarlet cloth. Price 50 cents.

HAPS AND MISHAPS OF A TOUR IN EUROPE. (Nearly ready.)

GEORGE S. HILLARD'S WRITINGS.

SIX MONTHS IN ITALY. 2 vols. 16mo. Price $2.50.

DANGERS AND DUTIES OF THE MERCANTILE PROFESSION. Price 25 cents.

MRS. JUDSON'S WRITINGS.

ALDERBROOK. By FANNY FORESTER. 2 Vols. Price $1.75.

THE KATHAYAN SLAVE, AND OTHER PAPERS. 1 vol. Price 63 cents.

MY TWO SISTERS: A SKETCH FROM MEMORY.

HENRY GILES'S WRITINGS.

LECTURES, ESSAYS, AND MISCELLANEOUS WRITINGS. 2 Vols. Price $1.50.

DISCOURSES ON LIFE. Price 75 cents.

R. H. STODDARD'S WRITINGS.

POEMS. Cloth. Price 63 cents.

ADVENTURES IN FAIRY LAND. Just out. 75 cents.

WILLIAM MOTHERWELL'S WRITINGS.

POEMS, NARRATIVE AND LYRICAL. New Ed. $1.25.

POSTHUMOUS POEMS. Boards. Price 50 cents.

MINSTRELSY, ANC. AND MOD. 2 Vols. Boards. $1.50.

GOETHE'S WRITINGS.

WILHELM MEISTER. Translated by THOMAS CARLYLE. 2 Vols. Price $2.50.

GOETHE'S FAUST. Translated by HAYWARD. Price 75 cts.

MRS. CROSLAND'S WRITINGS.

LYDIA: A WOMAN'S BOOK. Cloth. 75 cents.

ENGLISH TALES AND SKETCHES. Cloth. $1.00.

POETRY.

ALEXANDER SMITH'S POEMS. 1 vol. 16mo. Cloth. Price 50 cents.

CHARLES MACKAY'S POEMS. 1 Vol. Cloth. Price $1.00.

ROBERT BROWNING'S Poetical Works. 2 Vols. $2.00.

HENRY ALFORD'S POEMS. Just out. Price $1.25.

RICHARD MONCKTON MILNES. Poems of Many Years. Boards. Price 75 cents.

CHARLES SPRAGUE. Poetical and Prose Writings. With fine Portrait. Boards. Price 75 cents.

BAYARD TAYLOR. Poems. Cloth. Price 63 cents.

R. H. STODDARD. Poems. Cloth. 63 cents.

JOHN G. SAXE. Poems. With Portrait. Boards, 63 cents. Cloth, 75 cents.

HENRY T. TUCKERMAN. Poems. Cloth. Price 75 cents.

BOWRING'S MATINS AND VESPERS. Price 50 cents.

MEMORY AND HOPE. A Book of Poems, referring to Childhood. Cloth. Price $2.00.

THALATTA: A Book for the Sea-Side. 1 vol. 16mo. Cloth. Price 75 cents.

MISCELLANEOUS.

OUR VILLAGE. By Mary Russell Mitford. Illustrated. 2 vols. 16mo. Cloth. Price $2.50.

NOTES FROM LIFE. By Henry Taylor, author of 'Philip Van Artevelde.' 1 vol. 16mo. Cloth. Price 63 cents.

REJECTED ADDRESSES. By Horace and James Smith. Boards, Price 50 cents. Cloth, 63 cents.

WARRENIANA. A Companion to the 'Rejected Addresses.' Price 63 cents.

WILLIAM WORDSWORTH'S BIOGRAPHY. By Dr. C. Wordsworth. 2 vols. Price $2.50.

ART OF PROLONGING LIFE. By Hufeland. Edited by Erasmus Wilson, F. R. S. 1 vol. 16mo. Price 75 cents.

JOSEPH T. BUCKINGHAM'S PERSONAL MEMOIRS AND RECOLLECTIONS OF EDITORIAL LIFE. With Portrait. 2 vols. 16mo Price $1.50.

VILLAGE LIFE IN EGYPT. By the Author of 'Adventures in the Lybian Desert.' 2 vols. 16mo. Price $1.25.

PRIOR'S LIFE OF EDMUND BURKE. 2 vols. 16mo. Price $2.00.

PALISSY THE POTTER. By the Author of 'How to make Home Unhealthy' 2 vols. 16mo. Price $1.50.

WILLIAM MOUNTFORD. THORPE: A QUIET ENGLISH TOWN, AND HUMAN LIFE THEREIN. 16mo. Price $1.00.

MRS. A C. LOWELL. THOUGHTS ON THE EDUCATION OF GIRLS. Price 25 cents.

CHARLES SUMNER. ORATIONS AND SPEECHES. 2 Vols. Price $2.50.

HORACE MANN. A FEW THOUGHTS FOR A YOUNG MAN. Price 25 cents.

F. W. P. GREENWOOD. SERMONS OF CONSOLATION. $1.00.

HEROINES OF THE MISSIONARY ENTERPRISE. 75 cts.

MEMOIR OF THE BUCKMINSTERS, FATHER AND SON. By Mrs. LEE. Price $1.25.

THE SOLITARY OF JUAN FERNANDEZ. By the Author of Picciola. Price 50 cents.

THE BOSTON BOOK. Price $1.25.

ANGEL-VOICES. Price 38 cents.

SIR ROGER DE COVERLEY. From the 'Spectator.' 75 cts.

S. T. WALLIS. SPAIN, HER INSTITUTIONS, POLITICS, AND PUBLIC MEN. Price $1.00.

LIGHT ON THE DARK RIVER: OR, MEMOIRS OF MRS. HAMLIN. 1 vol. 16mo. Price $1,00.

RUTH, A New Novel by the Author of 'MARY BARTON.' Cheap Edition. Price 38 cents.

LABOR AND LOVE: A TALE OF ENGLISH LIFE. 50 cents.

MRS. PUTNAM'S RECEIPT BOOK; AN ASSISTANT TO HOUSEKEEPERS. 1 vol. 16mo. Price 50 cents.

EACH OF THE ABOVE POEMS AND PROSE WRITINGS, MAY BE HAD IN VARIOUS STYLES OF HANDSOME BINDING.

JUVENILE.

THE DESERT HOME, or, THE ADVENTURES OF A LOST FAMILY IN THE WILDERNESS. By Capt. Mayne Reid. With fine plates, $1.00.

THE BOY HUNTERS. By CAPT. MAYNE REID. With fine plates. Just published. Price 75 cents.

THE YOUNG VOYAGEURS, OR, THE BOY HUNTERS IN THE NORTH. By CAPT. MAYNE REID.

ADVENTURES IN FAIRY LAND. By R. H. STODDARD. With fine plates. Just out. Price 75 cents.

AUNT EFFIE'S RHYMES. With beautiful Engravings. Just published. 75 cents.

ELIZA BUCKMINSTER LEE. FLORENCE, THE PARISH ORPHAN; and A SKETCH OF THE VILLAGE IN THE LAST CENTURY. 1 vol. 16mo. Cloth, 50 cents; cloth, gilt edge, 63 cents.

MRS. SARAH P. DOUGHTY. THE LITTLE CHILD'S FRIEND. With illustrations. 1 vol. square 16mo. Cloth, 38 cents.

MEMOIRS OF A LONDON DOLL. Written by herself. Edited by Mrs. Fairstair. With engravings. 1 vol. square 16mo. Scarlet cloth, 50 cents; gilt edge, 63 cents.

TALES FROM CATLAND, FOR LITTLE KITTENS. By an OLD TABBY. With engravings. 1 vol. square 16mo. Scarlet cloth, 50 cents; gilt edge, 63 cents.

THE STORY OF AN APPLE. Illustrated by JOHN GILBERT. 1 vol. Square 16mo. Scarlet cloth. Price 50 cents.

THE DOLL AND HER FRIENDS; A Companion to the 'Memoirs of a London Doll.' With illustrations. 1 vol. square 16mo., 50 cents.

JACK HALLIARD. VOYAGES AND ADVENTURES IN THE ARCTIC OCEAN. With Engravings. 16mo. Cloth, 38 cents.

S. G. GOODRICH'S

LAMBERT LILLY'S HISTORY OF THE NEW-ENGLAND STATES. With numerous Engravings. 18mo. Cloth, 38 cts.

LAMBERT LILLY'S HISTORY OF THE MIDDLE STATES. With numerous Engravings. 18mo. Cloth, 38 cents.

LAMBERT LILLY'S HISTORY OF THE SOUTHERN STATES: Virginia, North and South Carolina, and Georgia. With numerous Engravings. 18mo. Cloth, 38 cents.

LAMBERT LILLY'S HISTORY OF THE WESTERN STATES. With numerous Engravings. 18mo. Cloth, 38 cents.

LAMBERT LILLY'S STORY OF THE AMERICAN REVOLUTION. With numerous Engravings. 18mo. Cloth, 38 cents.

THE SAME, in 3 Vols. Red cloth, gilt, $1.88.

PARLEY'S SHORT STORIES FOR LONG NIGHTS. With eight colored Engravings, 16mo. cloth, 50 cents; uncolored Engravings, 40 cents.

THE INDESTRUCTIBLE BOOKS FOR CHILDREN. Printed on strong Cloth, expressly prepared. Four kinds, viz.: Alphabet — Primer — Spelling Book — Reading Book. Each 25 cents.

THE FOUR PARTS, Bound in one Cloth volume, 90 Pictures, $1.25.

☞ Any book published by TICKNOR & Co. will be sent by mail, postage free, on receipt of the publication price.

TICKNOR & COMPANY'S stock of Miscellaneous Books is very complete, and they respectfully solicit orders from CITY AND COUNTRY LIBRARIES.

www.ingramcontent.com/pod-product-compliance
Lightning Source LLC
LaVergne TN
LVHW011207110826
845150LV00006B/1353

* 9 7 8 1 4 2 5 5 1 7 7 4 8 *